# VOICES
# IN THE
# HALL

high school
principals
at work

BY WILLIAM E. WEBSTER

Phi Delta Kappa Educational Foundation
Bloomington, Indiana

Cover design by Victoria Voelker
Photograph by Vladimir Bektesh

Library of Congress Catalog Number 94-69463
ISBN 0-87367-469-3
Copyright © 1994 by William E. Webster
Bloomington, Indiana

To my mother, Katherine Snee Webster,
and my brother, James A. Webster, Jr.
They would have been proud.

# table of contents

# preface

Writing this book has in many ways been reliving parts of the last three-plus years. Listening to the tape recordings of interviews has enabled me to transport myself back to principals' offices in Alabama, Mississippi, Georgia, Wyoming, South Dakota, and other parts of the country. As I recall these experiences, I also have been reminded of driving into a hail storm that forced us off the road in Arizona and a rainstorm in Alabama that quickly turned an ordinary interstate highway into a turbulent mountain stream.

It is difficult for me to express sufficiently my gratitude to and admiration for the many people who took time from their very busy schedules to meet with me and to conduct me through their schools. I also am indebted to the central office personnel who scheduled the meetings and, in several cases, furnished transportation enabling me to efficiently visit schools.

I am grateful that my university gave me a sabbatical to allow me to conduct an important segment of my interviews. I treasure the support that I received from long-time mentors — Dr. Robert Binswanger, chair of the Department of Education, Dartmouth College, and Dr. Ralph Mosier, retired professor, Boston University. I also appreciate that Dr. Ted Sizer of the Coalition of Essential Schools felt that my findings could make an interesting book.

And most important, I want to thank my wife, Beverly, whose collaboration, support, and work made the final product possible. I have many memories of the two of us in motels across the country, reviewing the day's interviews, recording key numbers, and planning the following day's work, which each day included interviews and a drive to the next community.

Conducting the research and writing this book have been truly wonderful experiences and have strongly reinforced my belief in the absolutely essential role that the high school plays in America today.

1

*chapter one*

# REDISCOVERING THE HIGH SCHOOL PRINCIPAL'S ROLE

Exciting and filled with energy, as diverse as the communities they serve, bound by tradition: all these describe America's high schools. Their principals are pragmatic and oriented toward solving problems. They are keenly aware of their communities, staff, and students and work very hard to address the needs of these key stakeholders. The energy, enthusiasm, and commitment of high school administrators are national assets; they should not be taken for granted but must be used judiciously to improve education for America's youth.

These impressions of America's high schools and their administrators evolved through visits and interviews in more than 150 high schools in 23 states and 7 countries. I visited high schools in crime-ridden cities, in posh suburbs, in the forests of the Northwest and the Appalachians, along California's scenic coast, and on the flatlands of the Great Plains.

This three-year study of the high school principal started informally. It grew out of my roles as a professor of educational administration at California State University, Bakersfield, a co-director of the university's Institute for the Study of Secondary Education, and a lecturer in the Phi Delta Kappa Educational Foundation Author Seminar Lecture series. These functions brought me into contact with administrators in a great variety of schools.

Students in California's master's degree and administrative credential programs are required to complete several field experiences that must be supervised by university faculty. Therefore a basic part of my job as professor is to visit schools. Often, in addition to addressing student issues on these visits, I have been able to interact with the administrators on the nature of their work and, particularly, about opportunities and challenges that confront them on a daily basis.

As co-director of the Institute for the Study of Secondary Education, I served as a consultant to secondary school districts in California and to a statewide organization composed of high school district superintendents. In these activities I had many opportunities to talk with superintendents, central office personnel, and building principals about topics I had been discussing with field supervisors. Also in this role I served as principal investigator of a major reform effort in one of the state's largest secondary school districts.

Additional opportunities to visit schools across the nation and in four foreign countries came from my work in the Phi Delta Kappa Educational Foundation Author Seminar Lecture series. My PDK hosts were most cooperative in arranging visits to high schools.

Much of the data I was amassing painted a different picture of America's high schools from that depicted in newspapers and magazines in recent years. The books, *Politics, Markets, and America's Schools* by John Chubb and Terry Moe and *We Must Take Charge* by Chester Finn, stated positions very different from what I was learning firsthand. Hundreds of hours in schools and continuing contact with those who work in schools presented no evidence that schools were dysfunctional institutions. I saw them to be noisy, boisterous, and at times littered, particularly at the end of the day; but I found no evidence of chaos and disorganization. Further, the notion that principals were powerless cogs in a bureaucratic wheel — controlled both by a large, insensitive bureaucracy and by the strictures imposed by collective bargaining — was being contradicted by what principals were telling me.

The data I was gathering proved so interesting and, I believed, significant that I determined to do a formal study on the role of the high school principal. I developed a 35-item protocol for interviewing principals and a 17-item protocol for interviewing central office personnel. Initially I had focused on the role of the principal as a decision maker, interaction with central office personnel in making decisions, and the related roles of teachers in the decision-making process. As the study evolved, I included questions in additional categories that would give insights into the role of the principal, such as the principal as an educational innovator and instructional leader and the principal's role in working with the community and students.

I bought a small tape recorder to record the interviews, at first being doubtful about its usefulness. However, not one interviewee hesitated to have the conversations recorded. The use of the recorder produced much more comprehensive results than trying to capture the information by hand.

## Gathering the Data

The initial sample consisted of schools in California and those located close to where I appeared as an author-lecturer. During winter and spring breaks at the university, I expanded this sample, ultimately extending it to a representative national sample during a sabbatical in the fall of 1992. Finally, with the cooperation of my university, I took additional time in the fall of 1993 to visit sections of the country not previously covered.

The study now includes each geographic region of the continental United States — New England, Mid-Atlantic, Southeast, Southwest, Midwest, Rocky Mountains, Far West, and Alaska. I also visited schools in Indonesia, the Philippines, Taiwan, Australia, Brazil, Canada, and Scotland. However, the findings of the study reported in this book are based on data gathered visiting schools in the United States, although I use an occasional quote or anecdote based on visits out of the country. The sample includes inner-city, small-city, suburban, and rural schools with enrollments varying from 120 to 3,400 students and an average size of 1,120. The ethnic distribution of students ranges from close to 100% minority to 100% white.

The oldest principal in the sample was 54, the youngest 32, and the median age was 43. Of those interviewed, 27% were women; and 18% of the sample had doctorates. The most typical college major was social studies education, followed by English education; only 5% indicated that their major was physical education and that they had taught that subject.

As I expanded the study to include a nationwide sample, I would simply telephone school districts, ask for the individual at the central office who had responsibility for secondary education, explain the nature of the study, and ask to interview at least two high school principals. Smaller communities, of course, often had only one principal. During subsequent conversations, I would get directions to the central office or the first school to be visited and ask for suggestions for an appropriate place to stay while in the community. I followed the telephone communications with a letter confirming details. In the scores of telephone calls I made to set up interviews, I was rejected by only three school districts, who either presented too many bureaucratic hurdles or failed to return telephone calls. In those cases, I simply chose to contact a similar system in the same region.

The general strategy for the visits was initially to interview central office personnel. I then would visit the high schools to interview principals. The site visit usually took between 90 minutes and three hours and consisted of the interview and, time allowing, a walk around the building. Although the principal often accompanied me on the walk, sometimes busy schedules prevented this and the vice principal or, occasionally, a student escorted me. I found that the building tour gave me many insights and much knowledge about how principals conduct business.

## Some Observations

I found principals to be very hard-working individuals committed to making their schools the best they could be. Their typical workday started about 7:00 in the morning, but many indicated that they got to school around 6:00. The workday usually ended about 5:00, with an average of three nights a week at some school function and often two weekends out of four at some school-related activity.

I initially planned to search for a model of the high school principal. However, this proved to be impossible. I found that, although similarities existed, how tasks were handled, how decisions were structured, and how principals related to parents, youngsters, and teachers were so different that I soon abandoned the search for a single model. I discovered that each principal managed the school almost exclusively based on past experience as a teacher and administrator. It was only the rare exception who cited a theoretical foundation for his or her behavior or referred to any of the vast literature dealing with the management of schools.

Although I focused on interviewing principals and central office personnel, I had opportunities to talk with students, teachers, and parents, which enriched my view of the high school as an institution. From the walks around the schools emerged the beginning of the title of this book — *Voices in the Hall*. And the voices were many and varied, as were the languages spoken. Snippets of conversations between kids, between students and teachers, between principals and teachers, between principals and students echoed through the halls. On more than one occasion while waiting for the principal, I would wander through the corridors near the office and students would ask, "Are you going to be our substitute today?" Or I would be approached by a security person who would very politely ask me, "Is there any way of being of assistance?" When I explained my presence, I had many interesting conversations concerning the school, the students, and the nature of the community.

During these waiting periods I was able to take a good look at the schools' trophy cases. Somewhere in each school — sometimes in an annex to the gymnasium, other times in the main entry — would be trophies, painted footballs and basketballs, signed baseballs, and batons denoting past athletic triumphs. And this was an international phenomenon. I saw similar displays in Indonesia, Australia, Brazil, the Philippines, and Scotland.

I also noticed — first casually, but then I looked for it — a plaque in memory of a student, in every case a boy, who had died while attending the high school; the plaque would indicate that there was an annual award in the boy's memory presented as an honor to a student who had achieved outstanding success in some area. I found these memorial plaques or trophies in every high school I visited.

Although a pep rally was a pep rally, whether in Wyoming or Alabama, each school had its own identity; and the principal would always remind me that "we're different, we're unique." Each school indeed *was* different, with its own staff, community, and student body. However, the energy, activity, bustle, and noise were present everywhere. When playing the tapes of the principal interviews, I became quite aware of the noisy backgrounds. In several schools, the principal would suggest that we wait until after the change of classes to do the tour. In other schools the principal would say, "Let's get out while classes are changing to give you a real feel for the school."

The great variety of memorable vignettes and anecdotes gave texture and depth to the visits. For example, in a city in Wyoming I arrived the second day of school. The principal was not in his office but, via an ever-present walkie-talkie, he was apprised of my presence and shortly appeared. He explained to me that in the first couple of days of school, he visited every class every period; and if I wanted to accompany him, it was okay. It was a sprawling campus, and he meant what he said. We dashed from classroom to classroom; and he did business all the way along, in motion all the time, talking about textbooks, supplies, and the upcoming pep rally, which, of course, required a different schedule that had not been plugged into the bell system. Our sprint about the school was interrupted temporarily as he shepherded youngsters back into classrooms and communicated with the office to fix the bell schedule. Somewhere along the line of this marathon through the school, my shoe became untied; and I was not able to tie it until we finally reached the last classroom.

In one school in the delta country of Sacramento, an unhappy student was being enrolled by her mother. The student made it clear in very loud terms that she hated all #@*&%#@ schools and she knew that this #@*&%#@ school would be as bad as all the rest. Her mother's efforts to quiet her were unsuccessful; the noise ceased echoing throughout the office only when a counselor took them into an office and closed the door. While this was going on, two very well-groomed young ladies were distributing Valentine cards to all the office personnel. However, that activity was interrupted by a fire drill, which turned out to be a false alarm pulled by one of the students.

In a small high school in California's Sierra Nevadas, a student was plaintively imploring her mother on a public phone just outside the office to come get her. While I was waiting for the principal, I jotted down the conversation: "Come and get me. I want to get out of here. I don't care where Daddy has the car. Call him up. Tell him I have to come home." Through the window in the principal's office shortly thereafter, I saw a pickup arrive; and the student ran to the truck, jumped in, and left. No checking out of the office. No clearing her unplanned absence with anyone. She was "out of there."

In a school in rural Utah, I was in the middle of the interview when a young woman burst into the principal's office to announce that she had just received a letter telling her that she had won a major scholarship enabling her to go to the university of her choice. The principal exploded out of his chair, came around his desk, and gave her a big bear hug; they briefly discussed the meaning of the scholarship, her family's reactions, and the wonderful opportunities it made available to her. After she left, he told me the family background, the university in which she hoped to enroll, and her career aspirations. His responses to my questions made it clear that he had helped her fill out the scholarship application form.

On the walk around a school in a capital city of a Corn Belt state, the principal took me into an English-as-a-second-language classroom composed entirely of Vietnamese students who, without any prior warning, had appeared for registration the day school opened. He told me that a local religious charity had arranged for more than 100 Vietnamese families to start life anew in this Midwestern community. He explained that he called an emergency faculty meeting and asked for volunteers to serve as ESL teachers for the 120 high school-age Vietnamese students who spoke not a word of English and whose most recent experiences were in refugee camps in Thailand. Two teachers volunteered; and I was visiting the classroom of one of these energetic, enthusiastic, devoted teachers. When I asked about training for ESL, the principal said it was all on the job. The atmosphere of the classroom was wonderful. The teacher asked the kids to greet me in English, which they did in an eager and humorous manner, fully realizing they were performing.

While on the tour of a large high school in suburban Phoenix, the principal got a message that he was needed in the office. He excused himself, and I continued talking to a teacher who was explaining the school's television studio and its use of a local cable channel. About 20 minutes later I went to the principal's office to thank him for his hospitality and found him measuring a young man for a varsity jacket. He explained to me that selling varsity jackets was a small business he had on the side.

A particularly fascinating stop was in a very small high school in the forests of the Kenai Peninsula in Alaska. The enrollment of the school was almost entirely students of Russian descent. The area had been homesteaded several decades ago by a group of Russian expatriates interested in preserving their culture and language. The boys and girls and most of the teachers were in traditional garb, and instruction easily moved between English and Russian. The building was K-12 with about 150 students, including 40 in high school. The principal informed me that many of the bilingual graduates had gone on to interesting and productive careers. Driving back to the main road some 25 miles away, I was able to see golden and bald eagles as well as ptarmigans. It was a visit to remember.

In a major Southern California city, I visited three inner-city high schools in one day. At each school, uniformed police officers were in the process of either returning a student who had been picked up earlier for questioning or picking someone up to be arrested or questioned.

I found that in most big inner-city schools, security precautions were ever present; and it was explained to me that these precautions were aimed at keeping non-students from coming on campus. Quite remarkably, however, I had no feeling of tension nor of a prison-like atmosphere in these schools. The relations between the principal and students were open and friendly, very similar to those found in suburban and rural high schools. On these inner-city walks, I was surprised by how many students the principals knew by first names; and I commented on how impressive this was. In each case I got approximately the same answer: "These kids have got to realize that we know them, we like them, and that we care for them. For many of these kids, the school is a haven because, unhappily, their neighborhoods are just not safe."

Two interesting anecdotes from a high school in a large city in the Deep South and another in a small city in the Great Smoky Mountains give additional insights into the idiosyncratic behavior of principals. During the walk through in the first school, I heard singing coming from the auditorium, which turned out to be a madrigal group's dress rehearsal. While we were walking down the aisle toward the group, the bell rang and the singers began to disperse. The principal asked the leader to conduct the students in a couple more numbers for their "guest from California," and I had my own private concert. When we returned to the office, the principal announced over the loudspeaker system that the madrigal singers would be coming to class late and would not need passes because she had detained them.

In a high school in the Great Smoky Mountains the principal had a large office with doors on three sides. Three students sat at a large table on one side of the room, and a large picture window looked out at the rolling, fall-colored mountains. However, the activity in that office reminded me of a waiting room in a bus station. It turned out he was helping the three students with math homework, and from time to time the interview was interrupted either by questions from one of the students or a comment from the principal. Two or three times a secretary cut through the office on an errand, and a vice principal walked through accompanied by a student. On more than one occasion a teacher or another administrator walked in unannounced and started a conversation. At the end of the interview the principal told me, rather unnecessarily I thought, that he had an "open-door policy."

## Presenting the Findings

The interviews were transcribed from tapes to a computer, and the comments were categorized and reviewed. These interviews reveal how the high school principal functions as an administrator. The results of studying this information appear in the following chapters and describe the variety of roles that each high school principal plays. Readers should get a sense of what today's principals are doing in schools, insights into the high school as an institution, and possibly some ideas on how to improve secondary schools.

The data presented in Chapter 2 deal directly with the principal and school-site decision making — the freedom he or she has in making decisions about personnel, curriculum, and school-site budgets. The chapter also discusses the development of site-based management and other pertinent issues, such as the influence of union contracts and affirmative action policies.

Chapter 3 addresses the role of the principal as a change agent and the nature of this role in the arenas of instruction, school improvement, and restructuring. This chapter describes how different principals see their roles as instructional leaders and change agents, from being passive observers to determined initiators of innovations and improvement efforts.

The material in Chapter 4 focuses on the principal's relations with the teacher as a leader, motivator, and supporter and presents the principal's strategies for motivation, the varying structures for teacher decision making, the status of teacher empowerment in the schools, and the principal's management style as it relates to teachers.

Chapter 5 presents data on the principal's strategies for relating to and dealing directly with students and stresses how important student success and a safe and orderly school campus are to the principal's job satisfaction.

Chapter 6 discusses the principal as a community leader. This chapter covers the many strategies principals use to work with the community and the great variety of community groups they work with. It also presents some creative ways principals have used to reach out to minority communities and their strategies to involve businesses, large and small, in the life of the schools.

Chapter 7 concludes the book with some personal observations about the study and its findings and some suggestions relating to school management that might be useful to practicing administrators and those in universities involved in preparing future school administrators.

I have organized Chapters 2 through 6 in a similar way. Each starts with the questions I asked, followed by the findings. The findings are presented largely as representative quotes and anecdotes. Each chapter then ends with some conclusions. I identify schools with enrollments under 750 as small, enrollments from 751 to 1,750 as medium-size, and enrollments of more than 1,751 as large.

# chapter two

# DECISION MAKER

The current movement in education to site-based management prompted me to probe how high school principals view their freedom to make decisions for their schools. Further, I wanted to find out if principals really did have too many limits placed on their decision-making authority by bureaucratic and collective bargaining restrictions. Though not planned, questions about their decision-making authority led many principals to talk about how they involved teachers in this process.

To get a sense of the degree of their decision-making powers, I first asked each principal to describe the nature of their relationship with the superintendent and with the central office. I then followed this with three questions dealing directly with the topic:

- "How autonomous are you as a principal?"
- "In what areas do you make the key decisions, such as in personnel, curriculum, and budget?"
- "How do collective bargaining and contract management impinge on your decision-making processes?"

## Relations with the Superintendent and Central Office

Several responses were similar to one from a principal in a large city in Oregon, who said: "The superintendent and the board have made it clear that this school is my responsibility. They don't supervise me very carefully, and I make the basic decisions as far as this school is concerned."

A principal of a large suburban California high school put forth a similar notion, saying, "I make all the decisions as they relate to this building."

In a small community in New York, another stated: "I set goals and directions for this school. They allow me a great deal of freedom to do what I think is best in the day-to-day operation of the school."

Principals often indicated the relationship of responsibility and accountability to independence. A principal in a South Dakota city responded, "As principal, within a broad district framework, I'm almost completely free to make decisions at this school; and I expect to be held accountable for them." Reinforcing this concept, a California administrator said, "I accept responsibility for the total operation of my building."

A principal in a college town in Colorado alluded to the role of the state, saying, "We are reasonably autonomous, but often state edicts will interfere with autonomy."

In California several principals mentioned the impact that state frameworks had on curriculum development. One principal in a small city in San Diego County captured the attitude: "The overall framework is established by state frameworks, but in specific strategies and methodologies we are autonomous. I have pretty free rein in developing electives. I would like more autonomy. The University of California requirements restrict our flexibility."

Several principals from different parts of the country answered similarly, with the following quotes indicating that central office direction is not necessarily formal:

- "They pretty much let us do our own thing. They let us make most of our own decisions." (Industrial city in Colorado.)
- "The superintendent lets principals run their schools. His management style is one that gives us a great deal of independence." (Mid-size city in Nebraska.)
- "The superintendent told me when I got the job, 'We're here to help you, but we are not going to be in your hair all the time.' As a result, we are very autonomous." (A small Vermont town.)
- "I've been in several other districts, and our autonomy here is second to none. The expectations of the district are high, and they give the support and resources we need to achieve whatever we are doing. And they let us do it." (Midwestern rail center.)

Three quotes indicated that not all principals had the degree of freedom that they desired and were frustrated by this condition. A principal in a mid-size city in South Carolina said: "Some people in the central office think they are there to dictate to me what to do. This causes real problems."

A principal in rural Oregon commented, "They try to control as much in the central office as they can and often demand changes, I think, just to show their authority."

14

A principal in a large high school in a historic Massachusetts town stated, "The superintendent really likes to feel in control and will second-guess us on personnel decisions even if we have done a thorough job on screening and interviewing."

An informal but significant variable in the degree of decision-making authority or freedom was that, in many instances, principals had been in place longer than superintendents, as indicated by the following remarks:

- "I have a good relationship with all my superintendents. But we've had several of them lately; and this means I give more leadership to the central office than I get from them, and they leave me alone to make decisions." (Large county system on Alabama's Gulf Coast.)
- "We have a brand new superintendent. It seems we as principals will be greater players and have more significant roles in our schools and also in the district. The new message is that the central office wants to be informed but not looking over our shoulder." (Mid-size city in Oklahoma.)
- "I take seriously the responsibility that I'm in charge of running the school, and I run it independently. I have been around a long time, and they understand what I'm trying to do." (Urban setting in Colorado.)
- "We have a brand new superintendent. We're not sure what her management style is yet." (Large city in Tennessee.)
- "We have a new superintendent, and he gives us quite a bit of latitude." (Large city in a Midwestern wheat state.)
- "Since we have a new superintendent and I have been here such a long time, I probably have more freedom than most principals do." (Small city in Oregon.)

Another factor influencing the principal's freedom to make decisions in many cases was the size of the district, as shown by the following representative comments:

- "We're a small district, and this is the only high school. Therefore, we develop our own curriculum and select personnel; and I'm in charge of scheduling the use of the building for community groups." (Small high school in a town in the Big Horn Mountains of Wyoming.)
- "This school is like a family. We make our own decisions as far as dress code, discipline policy, personnel, and instructional mate-

rials. Sometimes we involve the superintendent; but she trusts us, and we generally take stuff directly to the board." (Medium-size suburban high school in South Carolina.)

Although principals appeared clearly to enjoy freedom to make decisions, it is interesting to note that they wanted recognition and support from the central office. Particularly angry statements came from principals in California's San Joaquin Valley and an urban center in Tennessee:

- "There is a real lack of district office awareness of what is going on in this school. We have a lot of activities we invite them to — kids performing — and they never come. That really makes me angry. We have excellent drama and vocal music programs, and they never come to see them. They never come out to see what we are doing, and we are doing some great things. They just judge us on test scores and how many complaints they get."
- "No one from the central office ever comes out here. We've had groups from all over the country visiting our art program, but no one from the central office has ever come out to see what we are doing."

Many principals indicated their districts were moving toward site-based management, and it was beginning to influence the relationship between the principal and central office. In a city in South Dakota a central office manager stated: "We're working on a district restructuring effort focusing on site-based management, and over the next couple of years we plan on moving more decision making to the site level. That's going to take time and training."

Another central office person in Massachusetts said: "We have a strategic plan that is moving more decisions to the site level. Traditionally, all personnel have been hired centrally; but we're trying to move that to the site."

Other central office comments reinforced the movement toward decentralization:

- "Traditionally, this has been a very centralized district, but now we're moving toward site-based management; and in the future principals should have more freedom to make decisions, particularly in selection of personnel." (Mid-size North Carolina city.)
- "We're in the process of developing a districtwide plan for site-based management, and it should give more decision making to site administrators." (An Oklahoma college town.)

Typical comments from principals on the transition to site-based decision making follow:

- "We're in a period of transition. We are moving from a top-down central office, where they made most of the decisions, to site-based management, where we'll be making most of the decisions." (Medium-size urban/suburban high school in Florida.)
- "We have been very autonomous in the past. With the new strategic plan, there is an attempt to bring us together; but each school is organized differently, and we have the flexibility if we meet the outcomes [part of an outcome-based education effort] to develop our program the way we want to. We are organized very differently than any other school, and I'm sure it will stay that way. The district commitment to site-based management and shared decision making allows us this autonomy." (Medium-size urban Mississippi school.)
- "As we move to site-based decision making, it's a little murky just how much autonomy we have." (Large Colorado system.)
- "The district is becoming more and more decentralized, and we operate pretty independently." (Small Wyoming city.)

The movement to site-based management was not without its problems. One New Mexico principal noted: "As we move from top-down, central office control to site-based management, we are in a period of transition. Central office jobs are being cut, and this means there is a lot of tension and uneasiness. There is cooperation, but a lot of energy is going into people trying to justify their present jobs."

## Personnel Decisions

The area in which the overwhelming number of principals felt they should have — and in most cases believed they did have — almost complete autonomy was the selection and assignment of personnel. One of the clearer statements was by a principal from a large city in Nebraska: "I do all the interviewing and screening. We basically do all the hiring out of the building."

This was supported by the central office of the same district when one manager said, "The principals have final say on who comes into their buildings."

However, there seemed to be a general pattern, with the district office doing the paper screening and establishing the pool from which schools make their final selection. As one central office person in a small South Dakota city said: "The paper work is handled at the central office. The principal makes the decision. They are totally autonomous in whom they select."

In the same district a principal responded: "I do all the hiring here. We usually draw from the pool established at the central office; but if we do not get what we want there, we can recruit on our own."

A New York principal answered in a similar manner when he said: "Central office does the recruiting, establishes a pool, and then I interview and select the people who come to this school. I make the final decision about who comes here."

In a large Nebraska district a central office person noted: "Our principals are very autonomous. Central office does the initial paper screening; but the principals have the final say, subject to affirmative action. We don't have collective bargaining."

In some cases the hiring of personnel seemed to be an area in transition, as indicated by a suburban Los Angeles principal: "Traditionally, all personnel have been hired centrally. But we're trying to move that to the site."

Often a reduction in force and contract language would impinge on the principal's freedom, as evidenced in the following remarks by two principals in a large Mississippi school system: "I have the final word on who comes here to fill vacancies, other than mandatory transfers due to reduction in force." According to the second principal: "I have almost complete autonomy in selection of teachers. The only time I don't is if teachers have to be moved because of changes in enrollment. I've determined to make the important personnel decisions myself, because I'm here on site and know the needs of the school."

Along the same line, a South Carolina principal said, "I'm almost independent in the selection of personnel, but I may have to take someone who has to transfer from another school due to a reduction in enrollment — in line with the agreement with the union."

Often personnel decision making seemed to be informal with no established policy. One Oregon principal said: "They pretty much let us do our own thing. They let us make most of our own decisions. They screen at the district level, but we make the final decision at the site."

In many cases teachers and other staff members were involved in the decision-making process for personnel selection. A principal in an urban Massachusetts high school stated: "On personnel, candidates are interviewed and tested and graded; and when I have an opening, I go in and review the files. And then at the building, we have our own selection process involving the assistant principals and department chairs. I take everybody's input, but then I make the final decision."

Where principals did not have this autonomy to select personnel, they expressed some hostility, as noted by an administrator in a large high school in Tennessee: "We have very little freedom in whom we select. And that's a frustration for me, because I like to make my own decisions and be accountable for them. The central office really makes personnel decisions."

Several principals mentioned the contract as a limiting factor. A Wyoming city principal remarked: "In the selection of personnel, my freedom is limited subject to the union contract; but I can usually get whom I want. I have unofficial last word as to who comes into the school. I find loopholes to get whom I want."

Almost universally, principals had no control over staffing ratios due to established districtwide teacher-pupil ratios; and in some school districts, this was a very favorable ratio. In one New England suburb, departmental averages for the student-teacher ratio in the major academic disciplines — mathematics, English, science, social studies, foreign language — were not to exceed 90 students per teacher, and this was in the contract.

Principals in a large Nebraska district had quite a bit of freedom in the area of personnel, as evidenced by this statement: "We are largely a decentralized system. We do the hiring. We have a point system, and last year we got 2,500 points. A teacher is worth 20 points. For secretaries and support personnel, 1 point is an hour; so a full-time secretary would be 8 points. And we can devise our own staffing to meet our needs."

In a large Mississippi city, in a state without collective bargaining, a principal reported the following: "When I got this job, the superintendent declared that this would be treated as a new school and, therefore, every position would be vacant. I had the responsibility to evaluate present staff and make recommendations about who would remain in this building. And to fill the vacancies, I had total freedom. I hired 48 new teachers who volunteered to come here, and I kept 27. The district had to find places for those whom I decided not to keep."

Factors that influenced personnel selection were the district's obligation to meet affirmative action guidelines and the principal's desire to have the racial-ethnic balance of the staff match that of the student body. Racial balance was mentioned several times and in several states. As an example, one central office manager in Florida said, "When hiring, principals must also take into consideration racial balance."

In no school with substantial percentages of minority students did the percentage of minority teachers on the faculty equal the percentage of minorities in the student body. The principals in these schools were committed to improving the percentages. Although they did not see this as a limitation to their autonomy, they did see it as a significant factor influencing their recruiting and hiring policies. They were clearly encouraged in these efforts by central office personnel. A comment summing up this attitude came from a principal in an urban Mississippi school: "We have over 80% African-American students and only 35% African-American teachers, and we need more. But we find it hard recruiting because there are so many more opportunities for able black students today than there were two or three decades ago."

A California principal in a school with more than 50% Latino students made a similar comment: "We are trying hard to increase the numbers of Hispanic teachers in our school, and we recruit nationwide. But the colleges just don't seem to be producing enough minority students today who want to go into teaching."

## Impact of Collective Bargaining

Several states had no laws mandating collective bargaining, and it therefore was no issue. In states with collective bargaining, principals and central office people generally felt that the area on which collective bargaining had the greatest impact was the selection and placement of personnel.

Collective bargaining brought a variety of responses in the interviews. It tended to be more a factor at the central office than at the school sites in those states with collective bargaining, as indicated by the following central office comments:

- "Collective bargaining is a significant factor and guides us in many ways." (Large urban California district.)
- "Collective bargaining is important in this district. We have nine bargaining units. Unions and collective bargaining are part of the culture of this community." (Medium-size urban district in Wyoming.)
- "A real influence. We negotiate with teachers, administrators, and classified staff." (Medium-size city in South Dakota.)
- "Collective bargaining is a major factor. The union is controlled by old-guard conservatives; and they are suspicious of anything, including site-based management." (Large district in Bay Area in California.)

Although principals were aware of collective bargaining, it did not seem to be a significant factor in most districts. The comments that follow represent a majority of those responding to the question on collective bargaining:

- "Collective bargaining has no influence over what we do here."
- "Collective bargaining has absolutely no impact on my relations with the staff."
- "Collective bargaining — not really a major factor."
- "Collective bargaining really doesn't interfere with management of the school. We are aware of the contract and stay within it. It's really important to know the contract."

However, in a small number of the districts the interviews indicated collective bargaining was a significant factor:

- "Collective bargaining is a major factor. Particularly as we downsize, we really have to know and stick to the contract." (Small city in South Dakota.)
- "Things used to be very unpleasant, but lately we are getting along very well. It really does not impinge on the day-to-day relationship with teachers." (Small city in Southern California.)
- "In a way, I've never seen a teachers union as powerful as this one. I honestly believe they control the superintendent. They got the last one fired. I think this one is aware who has the power." (Medium-size Wyoming city.)
- "The teachers look very carefully at the numbers of hours worked each day, duty-free lunch, assured planning period. The union monitors very closely the transfer policy and its implementation. In setting up committees, I'm very careful to make sure I have the participation of the union leadership." (Medium-size urban district in Wyoming.)

Collective bargaining seemed to be considered as a benign influence in most districts or a major factor in some. However, two comments by principals indicated that collective bargaining could have a major negative influence on what happens in schools:

- "For several years we had students evaluate the Advanced Placement teachers in all subject areas; and the teachers and I felt that, although at times difficult, overall it improved instruction. An experienced and good teacher from another school moved in and was teaching in one of our Advanced Placement groups.

When she heard about student evaluation, she stated it was a violation of the contract and filed a grievance, which the other teachers had known about but ignored; and we were forced to abandon the practice." (Large suburban school in Southern San Joaquin Valley in California.)

- "I thought as principal I should set a model and assumed responsibilities for teaching a course in American history. A group of teachers filed a grievance stating the contract forbade administrators from teaching. I ignored them and continued to teach; but they took it to the board, and the board ordered me to stop teaching." (Large urban district in Massachusetts.)

## School Budget Decisions

The interviews indicated that the principals' influence on the budget appeared to be limited to instructional supplies and classroom materials. In all districts, the utilities, teacher salaries, and capital outlay expenses were district responsibilities. Typical answers of principals from different parts of the country on the budget question were:

- "We get a per-pupil amount for instruction, and that's under my direction."
- "Basically supplies and equipment."
- "We control all our supply and material money."
- "We have a formula for allocating money for schools, and we are autonomous on how we spend it."
- "I have control over everything but salaries and utilities."
- "Everything that is allocated to the school we control at the site level."

In some cases this expenditure included textbooks; but in other cases textbooks were omitted, as seen in the following statements:

- "I have control over local budget — and that's for textbooks and instructional supplies."
- "We get allocated a certain amount for each school, but it's just for supplies. Textbooks come out of a different funding source."

## Curriculum Decisions

Answers to the question about the degree of freedom to develop curriculum at the school-site level clearly indicated that, although districts involved their schools and teachers in developing curriculum, they saw this as a major district responsibility. The following comments amplify this point:

- "Our district is very centralized, particularly in terms of curriculum. We have teacher committees that develop curriculum and select texts. We have to follow the curriculum and use the texts." (Medium-size city in South Carolina.)
- "We have a countywide [district] curriculum. It's developed through a committee structure with representation of high school principals, vice principals, and teachers to set the curriculum for the district." (Medium-size city in Georgia.)
- "Principals must operate within the district's strategic plan. There is a lot of informal curriculum innovation at the site level; but we monitor it, and it has to be within the overall district plan." (Large district in California's San Diego County.)
- "Curriculum is a districtwide plan, and periodically each discipline comes up for review and change. The people who do this work are teachers." (Medium-size district in Great Smoky Mountains of North Carolina.)
- "Standard curriculum committees develop materials based on state regulations. Every committee has site representation. There are districtwide staff development committees to train teachers to go back to their schools to train other teachers, so we have some uniformity in curriculum." (Large district in Florida.)
- "Curriculum has been a centralized process becoming more decentralized, organized and controlled by districtwide committees. Curricula in schools have been carbon copies of one another." (Large urban district in Colorado.)

However, there appeared to be substantial flexibility given to sites:

- "Basic curriculum is by district committees, but schools can develop individual programs that must be approved by the central office." (Medium-size urban school in New Mexico.)
- "Curriculum is developed in a coordinated effort with representatives from all schools and involved offices in the district. The curriculum is based on the framework, so there is autonomy in this area; but in the implementation — teaching strategies, etc. — there is a great deal of latitude at the school-site level." (Large suburban Los Angeles school.)
- "Curriculum is a joint responsibility between the district office and schools, and we have committees in the four discipline areas. Schools can make individual course changes, particularly in the

electives area; but the overall direction and goals are set districtwide." (Large urban school in Nebraska.)

## Conclusions

The high school principal has a large degree of freedom to make key decisions in the school. This freedom is not necessarily total nor unfettered but, nevertheless, more than has been indicated in recent literature. The principal's freedom to make decisions often is influenced by the length of time he or she has been a principal and by the size of the district. Generally, the more senior the principal, the more freedom he or she has in making decisions; and the larger the district, the more the central office tends to develop processes that inhibit freedom to some extent.

At the site level a decision-making structure is often vague, and it is the principal who establishes the decision-making processes and boundaries. Most principals were quite explicit that they established the ground rules, if informally, for staff participation in decision making.

The high school principal has considerable authority in making personnel decisions that affect his or her school and usually feels this is sufficient.

Freedom in the area of curriculum is more limited, because in most cases curriculum guidelines are established at the district level, and this process also is influenced by statewide policies. However, the principals did feel that they had freedom to meet local needs and that the processes to develop elective courses were quite simple. In most cases, the principal felt comfortable with the degree of freedom, because district curricula are developed by committees on which schools are represented by teachers or administrators.

The principal's autonomy over budget usually is limited to funds allocated to the school for instructional supplies and classroom materials.

The movement toward site-based decision making, although in many cases in its beginning stages, is starting to become a significant element in managing schools, with the principal now receiving greater freedom in making decisions. In the movement from top-down to local decision making, the principal and central office seem to be searching for strategies to make the new system work to give the principal more decision-making authority at the site while providing the central office with authority for coordination and quality control.

Where there is collective bargaining, the principal is familiar with the union contract and works within the framework in making decisions. However, collective bargaining is considered at the central office to be a much more significant factor.

In schools where the percentage of minority students far exceeds minority faculty, principals are committed to bringing the ratios into closer alignment. As a result, although affirmative action did to some extent influence personnel selection, principals expressed no concern about this influence.

*chapter three*

# INSTRUCTIONAL LEADER AND CHANGE AGENT

To explore how principals see themselves as instructional leaders or change agents of their schools, I asked several questions related directly to these roles. Two questions, seemingly unrelated, gave further insights into the principals' viewpoints on change and their role as innovator.

I first asked each principal, "What is your primary goal as principal of this school?" Answers to this question often brought out their beliefs and commitments to innovation and change.

I followed this question with several queries directly related to instructional leadership and innovative efforts:

- "Do you consider yourself the instructional leader of this school?"
- "If yes, how do you implement this leadership?"
- "Do you have a written plan for instructional improvement?"
- "Do you have an instructional evaluation plan?"
- "Have you taken any leadership in developing programs you would consider innovative or reform oriented?"

During the interviews I asked principals what the most frustrating and the most satisfying parts of their jobs were. The responses fell into many areas of the study, but some of the answers about frustration clearly related to the principal's role as an instructional leader and innovator.

## Goals of the Principals

Very few responses to the question about the principal's primary goal emphasized the need for change. Most focused on student achievement, not necessarily calling for an improvement program but simply stressing that the key goal of the school was to see to it that students achieved success. Two very typical statements came from principals from a large system in Mississippi, who saw their primary goals as "having students leaving the school to become successful adults and productive citizens" and "I want this school to be an effective school where students can get a basic education so that they can function as productive citizens."

A principal in a small South Dakota town stated his goal, "I want to have young people leave here prepared to make decisions and be successful in whatever they choose to do, whether it's college or a job."

Many goals relating to student achievement were similar to the following:

- "To continue getting students prepared for college and addressing the dropout problem we have." (Large urban high school in San Diego County.)
- "To make sure that the program we offer allows the best education available. We want them prepared either for work or higher education. We want to meet the needs of kids from all segments of society." (Small suburban high school in Southern California.)
- "To ensure that we have an educational plan that is conducive to learning to give kids an opportunity to maximize their ability." (Medium-size urban Alabama school.)
- "To ensure that adequate instruction is foremost and available to all students." (Large urban high school in Nebraska.)
- "To share my vision of ideas with students and the community. I want everyone to know that the learning process is my goal." (Medium-size urban school in Arizona.)

Many had as their goals making the school a safe learning environment, as exemplified by the following statements:

- "To make the school a safe place where learning takes place." (Medium-size school in an Arizona college town.)
- "To keep the climate a warm, caring, learning environment." (Small Wyoming high school.)
- "To have this place a safe haven where kids feel safe and relaxed." (Large inner-city high school in California.)

Although most of the goal statements appeared to call for maintaining the status quo, some comments cited needs for improvement. A few of the principals stated very specific needs that might be termed as piecemeal change, as shown in the following examples:

- "Getting technology into the school." (Medium-size urban/suburban school in Florida.)

- "Increase our test scores, and get our SAT scores up to the state level." (Medium-size urban school in Georgia.)
- "Move forward each year in a positive mode that includes not only test scores but morale, attitudes, and perceptions." (Medium-size high school in South Carolina.)
- "Increase student expectations, decrease the dropout rate, and increase the number of students going on to higher education." (Medium-size urban/suburban high school in an industrial city in Colorado.)
- "Create an atmosphere of cooperation and staff collegiality." (Small high school in a rural Colorado city.)

They were few, but some principals had as their goals the introduction of substantive change and reform, though as yet with no effort under way, and are represented by the following statements:

- "Get the faculty not to say, 'We've never done it that way'." A sub-goal of this principal was "to get the staff not to rest on tradition but to look to the future." (Medium-size suburban/rural high school in Wyoming.)
- "Bridge all the communities that this school serves. We have a mix of very high socioeconomic communities and very low SES minority students. Bringing all these students together is tough, but this is my major goal." (Medium-size school in a multicultural community in California's Bay Area.)
- "Completely restructure this school consistent with the Coalition of Essential Schools Model." (Medium-size suburban Bay Area high school.)
- "Completely restructure the high school." (Small rural New Hampshire high school.)

Two principals had an ambitious, if rather vague, goal. One principal in Colorado and one in South Dakota said they wanted to make their high schools "the best" in their respective states.

## The Instructional Leader

Many of the principals answered positively when asked if they were the instructional leader of the school, but some were very clear that they did not see themselves in this role. Principals who made up a third group saw themselves as facilitators, delegators, and supporters of others in the instructional leadership function. The nature of the role seemed not to be based on any clear vision or theoretical framework, but rather as a function of the individual's personal view of how the job should be done.

All of the principals in the group below answered affirmatively when asked if they were instructional leaders, and the quotes are their responses to how they implemented this leadership:

- "I do this largely by a goal-setting process and mutually developing strategies with teachers. If a student has a failing grade, the teacher must have a file to show what interventions were taken to address that failure. But I do this through department chairs." (Medium-size urban school in Mississippi.)
- "I work to get teachers involved. We have a school reform committee that meets regularly. I also meet regularly with department chairs. We are just beginning these efforts." (Medium-size rural school in Mississippi.)
- "Through supervision and evaluation and also by participating in staff development programs both as a participant and leader." (Medium-size school in a small South Dakota community.)
- "I work directly with staff on curriculum development." (Medium-size rural high school in Northern California.)
- "I talk about curricular matters at faculty meetings once a month, and I have monthly meetings with teachers and bring them together during their prep periods and talk about ways to improve our school." (Large high school in a Los Angeles suburb.)
- "I have a faculty advisory committee and also a school cabinet. I also meet with department chairs once a month. Between these three groups, we deal with curricular issues." (Large urban high school in San Diego County.)
- "That is my major focus. I meet regularly with my school planning committee made up of department chairs, assistant principals, and guidance counselors. We don't have a real plan worked up, but we are working together." (Medium-size urban school in Georgia.)
- "Developing programs such as our School Reform Model. I encourage teacher initiatives, and I work with the staff to develop goals and objectives and then work further to develop programs to implement these goals." (Medium-size urban/suburban Colorado school.)
- "I begin by holding very high expectations. We have departmental meetings once a month, and here's where our major curriculum goals are established." (Small high school in a South Carolina city.)

- "By visiting classes and sponsoring inservice training." (Medium-size urban/rural school in Arizona.)
- "I review the teachers' goals with them regularly. I hold seminars where teachers get together and discuss such things as cooperative learning and cultural diversity." (Medium-size suburban high school in a college town in Colorado.)
- "This is my primary role. I make sure the staff is aware of the latest developments in their field. I work to get them additional resources and introduce new teaching techniques, such as cooperative learning." (Medium-size suburban high school in Arizona.)
- "I monitor instruction by regularly visiting classrooms and encourage teachers to take inservice training courses." (Medium-size inner-city school in Tennessee.)
- "Our community is changing since one of our new and major employers has brought new families into the community whose home language is other than English. I've been working with the staff to design ESL and other programs to help these students." (Small rural high school in Oregon.)

Two New England principals made comments that do not fit into any category. One said, "Well, maybe, kind of." The other said, "Yes, by indirection. I raise issues and hope they will seize the opportunity to improve."

Those who felt that being the instructional leader was not their role were emphatic in their beliefs. The strongest opposing view was offered by a principal in a medium-size high school in North Carolina, who stated: "This is a farcical question to ask the principal of any high school. If the school is organized properly, the department chairs are the instructional leaders. They are the people who are sent to the workshops to keep up with the latest trends in their departments. I hold them accountable for students' performance in their areas."

In a large high school in California's San Joaquin Valley, a principal said: "I don't believe a principal of a school this size can be the instructional leader. It's not possible. I have to depend on the assistant principal for curriculum and the department chairs."

In a Colorado district one principal said, "No, the experts are the department people; and it is from those folks that we will have the success we strive for."

A principal in Utah told me: "I have very little real time to devote to instruction. With all of the paperwork and demands on my time, I simply can't do it."

In New Mexico a principal answered similarly, "It is hard to be an instructional leader with all the other duties I have in a school of this size."

The principal in a small coastal town in California replied: "No. Department chairs take the responsibility."

Principals who saw themselves in the middle roles as facilitators, delegators, and supporters are represented by the following comments:

- "I delegate instructional leadership to a vice principal." (Medium-size urban school on Alabama's Gulf Coast.)
- "I would say yes, although the direct leadership is implemented by an assistant principal who is in charge of curriculum. I stay in touch by visiting classrooms." (Medium-size rural/suburban school in Nebraska.)
- "I think so. I try to be. But I have an assistant principal who concentrates on curriculum. But with our changing populations, I'm taking a more important role." (Large suburban San Joaquin Valley school.)
- "I see the department chairs as the key instructional leaders in this school, and I stay in touch with them. I see myself as a facilitator, helping department chairs and teachers getting done what they want to get done." In response to a follow-up question, this principal stated that there was no real structure for instructional improvement but that he did meet periodically with the department chairs as a group. (Large suburban/urban high school in Florida.)
- "Yes and no. I'm really a facilitator." Again there was no structure other than department chair meetings. (Medium-size suburban school in Colorado city.)
- "Yes, by setting the tone and atmosphere, although the actual leadership is carried out by the assistant principal and department chairs." (Large suburban high school in California's high desert country.)
- "No, but I see to it that the vice principal for instruction is working with department chairs." (Small city district in New Mexico.)
- "I consider myself one of the instructional leaders on the campus. We share in instructional leadership, and it's not just one person's job." (Medium-size urban/rural high school in Arizona.)
- "My responsibility is to give teachers the opportunity to improve. I try to be the catalyst to make sure they are up-to-date as to what is going on." (Small suburban school in Southern California.)

- "I'm one of the instructional leaders. I can't have all the ideas. My goal is to identify the ideas that come from the faculty and a process to implement them." (Medium-size urban high school in Wyoming.)
- "No, but I see to it that the vice principal for instruction is working with department chairs on instruction." (High school in a small rural community in California.)

Not being the instructional leader of the school appeared to be a source of frustration for some. As one principal in South Dakota said: "I do not have the time. That is my biggest frustration. I should be and I'm not."

In a district in Wyoming, one principal stated: "Not as strong as I would like it to be. I'm working on establishing relations to become the instructional leader."

In a large suburban high school in California's Antelope Valley, the principal said, "My time is consumed with other responsibilities, and my preference would be to use this time to work more on instruction."

In another medium-size high school in a Bay Area suburb, the principal stated: "The two major jobs of a high school principal are difficult jobs to do well if you try to do both. One is management. The other is instructional leader. But trying to do both, I probably don't do either as well as I should."

## Written Plans for Instructional Improvement and Evaluation

About half of the principals interviewed stated they had a written plan for instructional improvement, and about one-third of those who did not have a written plan indicated that they were working on one. In several states there was a state-mandated improvement plan; and in California several schools reported that the document prepared by the state education agency, titled "Second-to-None," would form the basis of their improvement plans.

About one-third of those who had a written plan said they had an evaluation plan to measure the effectiveness of the improvement plan. In no case, however, did they state that the evaluation was being conducted by a third party, such as a university.

Inconsistencies existed between the central office and schools. For example, in a district in California's San Joaquin Valley, when asked if the district had a plan for improvement, the central office person responded, "No, but we're beginning to think about it." When a similar question was asked at specific schools, however, the principals indicated that they did have plans leading to a restructuring effort.

More pronounced differences between the view of the central office and the school sites were represented by responses from a large district in New Mexico. When asked about district improvement plans, the director of curriculum responded, "Yes, we have a major districtwide restructuring program under way, and each school has its own plan that meshes with the district's strategic plan." When at the site, I asked the principal the same question, and he replied: "No, we do not. There has been a lot of talk, but as yet nothing has happened." I found similar contradictions in school districts in Colorado, Florida, Tennessee, and Massachusetts.

## Innovative Programs

When asked if they had taken leadership in any program that could be described as innovative or reform-oriented, the principals responded with as many variations as in the question on instructional leadership. Some indicated having taken no leadership in an innovative or change program. Others cited individual changes related to a specific phase of school life. A small minority described major restructuring efforts in which they had taken the lead.

Among specific innovations they had led, several principals cited involving local businesses and government agencies. For example, in a middle-size urban Georgia high school, the principal cited his "Students for Success Program," in which business donations were used to provide awards to students for perfect attendance and improvement of grades. In a large suburban high school in Antelope Valley in California, the principal noted the construction of a building in cooperation with city government as an innovative effort for which she was responsible. And in a large urban/suburban high school in Florida, the innovative program was a "Gifted Externship Program," where "gifted students leave the school and work with mentors in the health department."

Although the high schools that composed the sample were representative, principals rather infrequently cited the existence of programs to address the needs of at-risk students. A school in a large Midwestern city addressed the problem with a plan that culminated with the principal interviewing each exiting student, during which the principal assured the student that there would always be a welcome should the student choose to return to school.

A principal in a large district in California cited a major program that involved team teaching and parent involvement whose major focus was to encourage more students to go on to higher education and which had a sub-goal of reducing the number of dropouts.

The principal of a high school in a small city in Arizona said, "We have a team teaching program for high-risk students that I am responsible for."

In an Alabama system a principal responded, "Not innovative, but I've worked very hard at getting kids into classrooms and to stay in school." Added was the comment, "The degree of centralization makes local innovation almost impossible."

A development identified during the course of the study was the emergence of tech-prep programs. Tech prep focuses on providing education and career preparation for high school students who are not contemplating going directly to four-year degree-granting institutions. Tech-prep programs focus on preparing students to live in a highly technological society and to take their places in a new kind of work force that will enable the nation to compete in a global economy. An important part of the tech-prep effort is cooperation between high schools and community colleges on a sequence of courses leading to associate degrees.

Though not always the initiators of tech-prep programs (teachers usually initiated these programs), the principals I spoke to were enthusiastic supporters. Several of the principals I talked to had met each other at nationwide tech-prep meetings. California, Massachusetts, South Dakota, Alabama, New York, Nebraska, North Carolina, and Wyoming had operating tech-prep programs.

Principals reported a wide range of efforts to improve specific programs or the climate of the school: In a small South Carolina school, the innovation cited was elimination of study hall, for which the principal had taken responsibility. In a middle-size suburban school in North Carolina, the institution of a course structure titled "Progressive Performance" was a reasonably detailed tracking program that enabled good, hard-working students to complete by their senior year courses that were acceptable to the state universities. An incentive provided at a San Joaquin Valley school was that students did not have to take finals if they had an "A" average.

- "We instituted a program of 'Strategic Planning and Total Quality Management' that we believe is improving instruction in the school." (Small rural high school in Oregon.)

- "We are completely restructuring our technology effort, and we have created three new computer labs. I was the leader in developing the proposals that got us funding for these labs." (Small city in New York.)
- "We started a preschool education program that is part of our course in Early Childhood Education that I'm very excited about." (Suburban school in Massachusetts.)
- "Introduction of honors-level classes and an academic decathlon." (Large city high school in Utah.)
- "I've introduced a program of peer evaluation. We're starting small with a few volunteers, and I hope that it expands in the future." (Large urban high school in New Mexico.)

Four principals reported their innovative programs taking the lead in major restructuring efforts. A medium-size high school in the Four Corners area of Colorado had opted for a four-period day and a team-teaching program, and a second school was in the process of implementing a similar program. A medium-size high school in Wyoming was working with a university on a major restructuring program, as was another medium-size school in South Dakota.

Maintaining the status quo and supporting others in innovative programs were other options mentioned by principals. For example, a principal in an urban area of Tennessee stated that his aim was to maintain traditional programs. A principal in a large city in Florida said: "I've not done anything myself, but I have encouraged and helped others to do things. Frankly, our staff thinks it is doing really a great job and is not interested in doing anything new because it is satisfied with what it is doing."

## Conclusions

Instructional leadership and the principal's role as an innovator were areas where principals responded in so many different ways that no identifiable model or consistent strategies emerged. However, through responses in this phase of the interviews, I gained considerable information as to the status of change and improvement efforts in high schools.

Responses confirmed that most high schools throughout the country do have efforts of varying sizes and in different stages to improve the quality of education. Although some improvement-oriented activities have been well-publicized, such as the federal government's Goals 2000 reform legislation and Ted Sizer's Coalition of Essential Schools,

I found few schools where improvement efforts could be identified as major and fundamental restructuring programs. Improvement efforts reported by the interviewees appeared to be largely remedies for what individual principals saw as immediate and concrete problems, including anti-drug programs, tightening discipline, and abandoning traditional study halls.

Some rationale for the absence of fundamental restructuring might be found in responses to the question about the most frustrating aspects of the principal's job. A Colorado principal answered, "Meeting with staff resistance to change." This was echoed by principals in Arizona, Massachusetts, New York, Florida, and Georgia. Two principals, one in Wyoming and one in California, were frustrated by faculty groups who said, "We've never done it that way," or "We've always done it this way." Lack of time to work with staff, insufficient funding, and insufficient understanding and support from the central office often frustrated principals and inhibited change and improvement.

The different approaches to instructional leadership reflected the principals' views of the job, which went from embracing the instructional leadership role to rejecting it. The enduring and traditional organizational structure of the high school remained the norm, with the principal in charge of the school, though not the intellectual leader. In most instances, the department chair was the primary mover in instructional improvement.

The business community is emerging as an active player in school improvement efforts. Of the schools I visited, the most sought-after role for businesses was financial support for specific programs. This sector of the community often served as a source for mentors, and in several cases the business community conducted inservice training.

The absence of meaningful participation of institutions of higher education, including schools of education, in school improvement efforts is disappointing. However, the few administrators who did describe partnerships with universities spoke positively and with enthusiasm. The basis of the working relationship often was a reflection of long-standing personal friendships, rather than an organizational imperative.

# chapter four

# LEADER, MOTIVATOR, SUPPORTER OF TEACHERS

The principal's role as a leader of teachers is related to the role of instructional leadership. Several questions revealed the strategies and management styles of principals as they affect teachers.

I asked each principal a broad question: "How would you describe your relations with your teaching staff?" Because a principal's management style partially governs interactions with teachers, I then asked, "How would you describe your management style?"

To determine the principal's role in motivating teachers, I asked: "What are your strategies to motivate teachers to continually improve?"

As discussed in Chapter 2, teachers will have a greater part in the decision-making process as principals move toward site-based management. I therefore asked principals two questions on this topic:

- Do you have a system to involve teaching staff in making significant decisions relating to the operation of the school?
- If yes, what is the nature of that system?

I also asked two questions about what were the satisfying and frustrating parts of the job in order to furnish more data about principal-teacher relations.

## Principal-Teacher Relations and Management Style

As with so many of the findings that emerged in the course of the study, the principals' answers to the question about their relationship with the staff covered a wide range. When describing the quality of their relationship with teachers, principals often were describing their management style; and the answers to the specific question on management style often were elaborations on the response about their relationships with teachers. Answers to the question on staff relationships, while indicating a developing movement toward participatory management, also confirmed that the traditional role of the principal as the final arbiter still was very much alive.

Examples of positive responses and some of the qualifications follow:

- "I have a good working relationship. We're working toward shared decision making." (Small rural New Hampshire school.)
- "We have a wonderful relationship. We know what we are here for, and we work together." (Medium-size urban high school in an industrial community in Massachusetts.)
- "We have good relations, and I feel that staff relations is one of my strongest points." (Medium-size suburban school in Oregon.)
- "Relations are good. We meet regularly, and the discussions are open." (Large urban school in New Mexico.)
- "We get along pretty well. The staff expects me to make decisions and be supportive, and I think I do and I am." (Small high school in an Oregon lumber town.)
- "Excellent. One of my major objectives is to involve the staff in decision making. We have an advisory committee, but I make the final decisions." (Medium-size rural/suburban school in Nebraska.)
- "I have a good relationship, but I am authoritarian." (Medium-size urban Tennessee school.)
- "I'm a new principal. I'm trying to change the culture of the school to a more open, participatory management style; and I've been getting good vibrations." (Medium-size high school in Colorado.)
- "We have good relations. I've lived in this community all my life, as have many of the teachers; and we get along. They know that I'm not afraid to make tough decisions, and I do." (Medium-size Utah city school.)
- "We're in the process of developing a program of site-based management, and this appears to be improving morale." (Medium-size Phoenix suburban school.)
- "I have excellent relations. I've been here a long time. I know the staff, and they know me. I'm not afraid to make the tough decisions, and they appreciate that." (Large urban school in California.)
- "Good relations. Two-way communication, and I spend a lot of time in classrooms meeting with and talking to teachers." (Medium-size suburban school in New Mexico.)
- "Improving. Last year it was rocky, and this year it is getting better by the day. I'm an agent for change, and this caused some real

troubles last year. This has been a very traditional school. I was an outsider. The intensity of the opposition was a real surprise." (Medium-size suburban/rural high school in Wyoming.)

Responses from three principals furnish evidence of how very different are the working environments in schools. One, a principal in a major city in Mississippi said: "It's developing. When I got this job, they declared every position in this school vacant; and I had the responsibility to evaluate present staff and recommend who would remain. I hired 48 new teachers and kept 27, and the district had to find places for the others. We're working hard to unify the new faculty with those who were already here, and I feel that we are making progress. I'm working to build trust, to raise expectations, and to get us to agree on some goals." In response to an additional question, this principal informed me that the district did not have collective bargaining, nor did the state have laws enabling teachers to gain tenured status.

The principal of a large high school in an agricultural center in California explained his relations with staff: "For the most part, we have good relations. This is a strong union site, and there are problems with active members. I've been working hard through staff development to get the staff to see the school is changing — increasing minorities — but we are making progress. Frankly, I've been combating the union by empowering teachers — using empowerment to beat the union. Shared decision making is a way to neutralize the union." (This was one of two occasions that a principal used the word "empowerment" in the course of the study.)

Describing a very different set of conditions, a principal in a small, isolated community in rural Alaska responded: "We don't really have a structure; but our teachers' room is where we socialize, and often our parents join us. We discuss a variety of issues, and sometimes these emerge as decisions that affect the school. It's very much like a family discussing vacation plans. Everybody has something to say, but eventually we reach a consensus."

A few principals did indicate their relations with teachers had trouble spots, as shown in the following examples:

- "A majority of the teachers appreciate me, and we work well together. I believe in adhering to state rules and regulations, and one of my jobs is to make sure that the teachers do. Some would rather just do what they want to do, and these people resent my enforcing the rules." (Large suburban/urban school in Florida.)

- "Relationships are strained. I was hired to 'reform' the school, and the movement toward shared decision making and greater teacher involvement is running into real resistance." (Small rural New England community.)
- "For the most part, relations are pretty good; but I had some real problems with some staff when I first got here. I'm trying to work through it with all of the staff." (Large urban school in a California coastal community.)
- "Overall, the relations are good; but there are some real malcontents who hurt the morale of the school." (Medium-size school in Nebraska.)

Responses to the question about management style reflected changes as schools moved toward involving teachers in the decision-making process. Again, their answers often reflected the dual role many principals saw for themselves as both the facilitator/supporter and the person who makes the final decision. Some examples of these comments follow:

- "Open, encouraging, supportive." (Medium-size urban school in Alabama.)
- "Shared decision making and involvement." (Medium-size urban Georgia school.)
- "Participatory management. But I don't hesitate to make decisions that have to be made." (Medium-size urban school in South Carolina.)
- "Personalized, first-name basis, cooperative, collegial." (Small high school in an agricultural city in Colorado.)
- "Open, non-confrontational, consensus building." (Large urban school in Nebraska.)
- "Democratic, participatory, but I make the final decisions." (Medium-size school in a South Dakota city.)
- "Very open. I make the final decision. But before making that decision, I'm very open to staff." (Large urban high school in California's northern San Joaquin Valley.)
- "Leader, manager, focuser, and director of people." (Medium-size urban school in Colorado.)
- "Director-paternalistic." (Medium-size city in North Carolina.)
- "Directive, but I listen." (Large inner-city school in Tennessee.)
- "Humanistic, collaborative." (Large suburban school in California's high desert.)
- "Director, supervisor." (Medium-size urban school in Mississippi.)

In addition, there were many who valued the "management-by-walking-around" (MBWA) approach and emphasized that a key element in their style was continuing visibility in classrooms, corridors, and cafeterias.

Two principals in Florida managed mostly on an individualized, flexible basis:

- "Depends upon the teacher. I try to be a good listener, supporter, cheerleader, mentor, coach to faculty. For some teachers needing help, I'm very directive and controlling. I try to build consensus on key issues."
- "Situation and flexible. Basic style is being directive. I try to give people autonomy to move off on their own."

The second time empowerment was specifically mentioned was in a small city in New York, where the principal said, "I manage this school by empowering teachers to come up with ideas, suggest improvements, and participate in making important decisions in this school."

## Motivating and Supporting Teachers

Answers to the question about motivating and supporting teachers ranged from brief to quite lengthy. Fitting the "very brief answer" category were two responses: "None." "No real strategy."

Other answers to this question fell into roughly four categories. A large number used supervision and evaluation as important motivational strategies. Mentioned frequently as a prime motivation technique was the positive reinforcement offered by principals after classroom visits. Typical responses in this category follow:

- "By monitoring classroom teaching and praising what I see." (Medium-size urban school in Tennessee.)
- "By classroom visits — supervision, positive reinforcement." (Another medium-size urban school in Tennessee.)
- "Through district inservice and evaluation." (Large suburban/urban Florida school.)
- "Through classroom observation and conferencing." (Rural school in a small Colorado town.)
- "I use evaluation very positively." (Medium-size school in Sacramento Valley town in California.)
- "I use the districtwide evaluation process and make four or five observations a year. I use the conferences to motivate, too." (Medium-size school in a small Arizona town.)

- "I motivate by using the clinical supervision model of evaluation." (Large suburban high school in Southern California.)
- "Continuing classroom visitations as part of the district evaluation policies." (Medium-size urban high school in New Mexico.)
- "By providing them with support, supervision, and inservice." (Large suburban high school in San Joaquin Valley.)

A second strategy for motivation was involving teachers, although these principals did not use the word "empowerment." Principals in both large and small high schools used this technique. Here are some typical answers:

- "Getting teachers involved in the goal-setting process and having them come up with ideas we can implement." (Medium-size rural high school in Mississippi.)
- "By giving teachers autonomy to work creatively in the class-room." (Medium-size urban school in Alabama.)
- "Simply by keeping them involved." (Medium-size suburban school in North Carolina.)
- "By giving teachers responsibility." (Medium-size suburban high school in Colorado.)
- "By getting them involved in our faculty advisory committee." (Large urban high school in Southern California.)

Inservice training made up a third category. Many principals mentioned inservice training both within the school and district and outside the district as a major motivator of teachers. The following examples are representative of what principals talked about:

- "We bring in good people for staff development in the building and give teachers opportunity to attend meetings for growth outside of the building." (Large suburban/urban high school in Florida.)
- "I encourage teachers to attend inservice training activities for specific purposes." (Medium-size suburban/rural school in Wyoming.)
- "Our primary method to motivate teachers has been by staff development, visits to other schools, and conferences." (Large urban high school in Utah.)
- "We have a strong staff development program." (Medium-size suburban Northern California high school.)

The last category of motivating techniques involves using incentives. Some principals explained how they involved local businesses in their encouragement strategies. A few samples of the creative ideas follow:

- "I reward teachers by giving them recognition. I recommend them to the local universities to supervise teachers or actually teach at the university." (Large urban school in Alabama.)
- "Recognizing good things that are done. Acknowledging these things publicly." (Medium-size urban high school in Wyoming.)
- "We have a variety of incentives. I continually send letters of support. We have gifts for teachers who do extra things that are supplied by the local businesses — say for 'teacher of the month' or 'teacher of the year.' Businesses will help us fund sending deserving teachers to conferences outside the district." (Medium-size urban school in Georgia.)
- "Through recognizing teachers, rewarding them, and through letters of commendation." (Medium-size urban high school in Colorado.)
- "Notes and letters." (Medium-size urban school in South Carolina.)
- "Students select a 'teacher of the week,' and the winner is treated to dinner for two at one of our local restaurants." (Medium-size suburban/rural school in Wyoming.)

Many principals told of their one-on-one and supportive relations with teachers to motivate them to strive to do their best. These personal efforts appeared in both very large and smaller high schools and in all parts of the country. Some of the principals' comments below reflect what many other principals said:

- "A one-on-one relationship. Supporting teachers particularly to reach personal goals." (Medium-size high school in rural Colorado.)
- "Taking time on a regular basis to talk individually to teachers about their concerns, goals, and strategies to reach those goals." (Medium-size rural/suburban school in Nebraska.)
- "I try to make them feel good, compliment them, recognize them, develop a personal relationship so I can be open and candid." (Medium-size school in a small South Dakota city.)
- "By establishing a one-on-one relationship and providing resources to help them get the job done." (Medium-size school in South Dakota.)

45

- "I make sure the teachers know I care about them. I don't really have a motivation strategy, but I'm supportive and get to know them as people." (Large suburban high school in Southern California.)
- "I support them and make them understand that their job is important. I provide them with the support they think they need." (Medium-size suburban school in Oregon.)
- "I encourage and support them and provide resources so they can do a better job." (Large urban school in Nebraska.)
- "I support people who are applying for individual programs of staff development." (Medium-size urban school in Wyoming.)

## Structures to Encourage Teacher Participation

The question about structures to involve teachers in the decision-making process produced a variety of responses. The centrality of the role of the department chair again emerged, as it did in the discussion about instructional leadership in Chapter 3. However, those principals who said they used the department chairs as the decision-making structure often indicated that the process was informal and operated on an ad hoc basis. The department chair was the only decision-making structure in a South Carolina community, in a high school in North Carolina, and in several schools in California, Utah, Arizona, and New Mexico.

The following principals' statements are typical of those who referred to the informality of a structure for decision making:

- "Through faculty and department meetings only. We don't really have a formal decision-making structure." (Medium-size urban school in Mississippi.)
- "Through department and grade-level meetings, but it's really casual and ad hoc." (Medium-size urban school in Alabama.)
- "No real strategy. Continual and informal contact." (Medium-size school in a small New Mexico community.)

Many schools seemed to be in the process of developing structures to involve teachers. The principal in a large California system voiced what many said: "We are beginning to involve teachers in a shared decision-making model. We have just started a restructuring committee made up of administrative staff, parents, students, and representatives elected by teachers. This is the policy group for the school. I do have veto power; but since we really discuss things, I've not had to use it."

Often committees would form to handle specific issues on an as-needed basis. Several schools reflected the response of a principal in New York who said, "Teachers are not involved formally, but we develop groups to make decisions on those things that affect them, like our Technology Committee that will make recommendations on the purchase of equipment such as computers and CD ROM players."

One principal in a city in Memphis said: "We have a group of committees. Teachers are not as involved as they think they should be, and I get criticized for it."

A principal in an Alabama community spoke of a special way of working with the school's advisory committee: "I meet regularly at a local restaurant with my advisory committee. We discuss major issues, and they make recommendations to me. Through my principal's fund, I pick up the tab. It's a dinner meeting, and the restaurant gives us a special deal. Meeting like this in a restaurant enables us to talk things over in a very nice environment. How often do teachers meet like this and have a meal paid for? Not very often."

Another principal in a large high school in a Colorado college town said a school governance group was in the process of being organized. The group would comprise teachers, students, and parents; and he saw himself as having only one vote and that vote equal to other members of the committee. He added that he saw himself also serving as the group's advisor, helping them to understand Colorado school law and district policy to ensure that decisions were made within existing frameworks.

Principals also reported school advisory committees as the formal structures in Georgia, Wyoming, California, and Colorado. Several schools in California used a school-site council as their decision-making body, and schools in Colorado and Florida had school improvement teams or committees. A school in Colorado had a site-based shared-decision-making committee. In several states, including Colorado, Oregon, and Massachusetts, school-based advisory groups recently had been mandated by state law. They were just in the process of being organized during my visits and were not entirely operative.

In other states where advisory groups were not mandatory but just getting under way, the principals indicated that they were experimenting. They all seemed confident that the groups would grow in power and influence. However, they almost always indicated that, because of their responsibilities, they had to reserve for themselves the ultimate decision-making power.

The principal in a rural part of Colorado described his school's planning teams: "The faculty is divided into four groups. The administrative staff meets with each of the four groups every other week for the purposes of curriculum planning and evaluation."

The principal in a valley school in Northern California described a faculty advisory committee: "It is made up of five teachers and two classified employees. Issues are brought to them. We talk about them. We work on such things as tardy policy and budget decisions." A school in Nebraska had a similar group, a faculty council, for overall policy setting.

Variations of the principal's council appeared in many schools throughout the country, usually made up of the principal and department chairs and divided into special-issue committees.

Probably the most complicated structure was in a large high school in South Dakota. The principal explained: "We have three decision-making teams. First, department chairs, and they serve as the instructional leadership team and meet monthly with me. The Faculty Council, selected by the faculty, deals with maintenance issues such as cleanliness and order. The School Improvement Team is the restructuring team that deals with major service efforts. This group directs the use of modernization project money from the state. I sit in on this but am not the director of this group. This group is really the trend-setting, direction-setting group for the school."

Most principals recognized that a major problem in involving teachers in the decision-making process was providing time. "It's difficult to schedule time during the school day to bring teachers together to make plans and decisions." This statement by a principal in Arizona was repeated by principals in almost every state visited.

Several schools were finding solutions to the time problem. In a large high school in New Mexico, teachers on the advisory committee were assigned to the same lunch to provide meeting times. In a large high school in South Carolina, department chairs, who were on the school's advisory committee along with the principal and vice principal, were free from first-period duties, which enabled the weekly morning meeting that was started before school to continue into the school day. A high school in Massachusetts and another in New Hampshire made teacher involvement easier by assigning teachers only four teaching periods out of seven, thereby allowing easy scheduling of meeting time for teachers during the day.

Several principals stated: "It's hard to get teachers involved when they teach five periods and have a load between 150 and 200 students. Meetings take time away from preparation and correcting papers."

## Most Satisfying and Most Frustrating Aspects of the Job

The array of answers to the most satisfying and frustrating aspects of the job showed how important personal relationships with teachers were to most principals. Some found their relations with teachers to be the best part of the job, while a few indicated that some individual teachers caused their greatest frustrations.

On the positive side, here are some uplifting comments to the most satisfying part of the principal's job:

- "Interaction with teachers. I really enjoy working with them." (Medium-size urban school in Tennessee.)
- "Seeing teachers succeed." (Large Utah high school.)
- "Working with teachers who are improving and using an increasing variety of teaching strategies." (Medium-size urban school in Mississippi.)
- "Seeing good things happen in the classroom." (Medium-size high school in Wyoming.)
- "Assisting professional teachers to grow and to develop." (Large urban school in Nebraska.)
- "Seeing a teacher getting turned on and becoming enthusiastic and doing a better job." (Medium-size suburban school in a California valley town.)
- "To see a new teacher blossom and begin to do an outstanding job." (Small city in Utah.)

The following responses are representative of what principals said about frustrating parts of the job:

- "It is difficult to motivate veteran teachers. It's tough to get the older teachers to change. The older ones let new ideas go right by. There are a couple we are just letting slide by until they retire." (Suburban high school in San Francisco Bay Area.)
- "Teachers who have blinders, who are narrow-minded, who won't look at the bigger picture." (Medium-size New Mexico high school.)
- "Working with a teacher who doesn't want to be here but stays anyway." (Medium-size urban school in South Carolina.)
- "Meeting with staff resistance to change." (Medium-size urban school in Colorado.)
- "Teachers who are satisfied with the way things are and don't want to change and particularly don't want to use new technology." (Small school in a Massachusetts community.)

49

- "I found the rift teachers believe exists between teachers and administrators frustrating. I'm also frustrated by a poor work ethic and hiding behind the union." (Medium-size suburban school in Wyoming.)

## Conclusions

The interviews indicated a nationwide movement toward shared decision making in schools, often created by state mandates. They also confirmed that principals often feel that since they are held responsible for what happens in schools, they also must have the final authority, calling into question just what teacher decision making means in actuality.

In most cases, the structures that allow greater teacher involvement are in a state of development. The nature of these structures often is based on the personality and past experience of the individual principal, rather than resulting from careful planning and thoughtful development; therefore these structures may appear to be informal and ad hoc.

Good relations with teachers are important to the principal, and a large measure of job satisfaction relates to the success of individual teachers. However, it appears that many principals have not given serious thought to motivating teachers. Strategies seem to be personal and casual, with heavy reliance on supervision as a motivating strategy.

Often the principal has not thought through his or her management style; and many principals appear to have no personal, coherent, and consistent leadership strategy. Their styles could best be referred to as crisis management, rather than a coherent set of interrelated experiences.

# chapter five

# MANAGER OF
# STUDENTS

Educating young people is the reason for schools. Thus how principals relate to students is an important component of the study. The answers to my questions in this area reinforced my belief in the importance of this relationship.

First, I asked two specific questions:

- "In what ways do you interact with the students?"
- "What are the major discipline problems in your school?"

A third question, though not directly oriented toward relationships with students, often brought out further information about these relations:

- "What qualities or characteristics would you describe that make your school different from any other?"

The three questions about the principal's primary goal, the most satisfying aspect of the job, and the greatest frustration of the job produced many answers that added to the data about the principal's interactions with students.

## Strategies for Interaction with Students

The responses to the first question about how the principal interacted with students furnished a great deal of information on how important principals felt it was to spend time relating to and working directly with students. Although this interaction usually was not formal nor structured, it was an activity to which most principals intentionally devoted time and effort.

The most consistent way principals interacted with students, as with teachers, fell under the term "management by walking around," followed closely by attendance at the great variety of school activities. Here are several answers that are representative of many others:

- "I probably spend more time communicating with kids than anything else. I'm a fanatic about that. My interactions are casual — before school, in the corridors, at lunch, after school. I go to athletic events and other extracurricular activities." (Large suburban high school in the Los Angeles area.)
- "I spend time in the hallways and in classrooms. I go to school events." (Medium-size inner-city high school in Tennessee.)
- "I spend a lot of time in the hallway. I also spend time in the classrooms, particularly laboratory classes that give me a chance to ask the kids what they are doing. I talk to kids before and after school and at their lunch hour." (Large suburban/urban school in Florida.)
- "I'm visible. I attend almost all activities, and I'm in the hallways between classes." (Medium-size urban/rural school in Arizona.)
- "I'm in the hallways, and I attend student activities. I go on field trips with them and attend all athletic events." (Large urban school in Nebraska.)
- "Interaction with kids is a major priority." (Medium-size city in New York.)

In addition to these continuing informal strategies, several principals had planned activities that brought them into contact with students. Though not typical, some principals said they met regularly with the student council, although in most schools this job was assigned to an assistant or vice principal. One principal said he taught a class called "Student Leadership." Another reported that she regularly sang "Happy Birthday" and delivered cards to the students.

A principal in a large Colorado city explained his different way of interacting with youngsters: "I carry a camera around with me and take pictures. I put them on the bulletin board; and at the end of the year, I have a slide show. Kids really like it."

In another Colorado city of medium size, the students were members of the school's improvement team. "Last year when implementing a new program, our administrators went into every classroom to talk to kids about upcoming changes. I also have a 'Pizza Forum,' where once a month I meet with a random selection of kids to discuss any issue in the school."

A principal in a small Georgia city had what she called a "Chat-o-rama." "I meet regularly in my office with a random sample of students, ensuring that there are good students as well as not-so-good students. I have food for them, and we just chat about the school."

In a school in South Dakota, the principal reported: "We have a team of administrators and counselors who meet weekly to review individual students who may be having problems, and together we design a strategy to help them out. And when we design strategies for particular youngsters, the teachers of those youngsters are involved in developing those strategies."

In a small community in Vermont, the high school principal told me he held regular retreats with students at a nearby camp resort. "In attendance will be 30 to 40 kids, counselors, parent volunteers, and myself. We spend from Friday night to Sunday afternoon; and it is a mix of games and recreation, including time discussing issues that have significance for teenagers, such as breaking up and dealing with poor grades. The program is designed so that in the four years of high school, each student has an opportunity to participate in the school-sponsored retreats. I really feel these retreats give me an opportunity to get to know each student in a personal way."

Several principals stated that serving as a substitute teacher was a strategy they used to get to know youngsters better. One California school had a formal program in which each administrator in the high school had to substitute at least 25 times a year. The principal reported that though the program was initiated for budgetary reasons, it worked out so well that it became a regular part of the administration of the school.

In a New England high school, students were part of the legislative arm of the school governance system that also included parents and teachers.

Two principals in California mentioned that they used the school's weight room for their own exercise and in this way got to interact informally with students. Another California principal in a rural area told of the community's monthly cleanup program where they rake and trim shrubs. He recruits students to participate in this program and also joins in the work.

One principal had what he called a "Pride Program." "Each month students who have done particularly well in either grades or attendance are identified, and I take them to lunch at a local pizza parlor that contributes the lunches."

Several principals mentioned reviewing quarterly and semester grades and meeting individually with students who were doing very well or were failing.

A major strategy of many principals was visiting classrooms. A large number of administrators said that although they visited classrooms to observe instruction, an important and almost equal reason was to observe and get to know students better.

A principal in Oklahoma had a student forum scheduled immediately after school once a month. "It is open to all students and provides an opportunity for a no-holds-barred discussion on any issue the students choose to raise."

In walking around the school with the principals, I observed their obvious personal knowledge of and efforts to communicate with kids. They continually interacted with students, asking such questions as: "Have you heard from your brother in the Gulf?" "Don't forget to let me know when you hear about your scholarship," "Don't forget we have a date after school tonight" (the principal was tutoring the student in math). Very often principals would introduce me to students with such comments as, "This is the third student we have had from this family."

Although almost every principal gave evidence of specific ways that he or she interacted with students, two principals stated that, by the nature of their jobs, they had very little contact with students. One principal in South Dakota stated: "This is a large school. We have several major change efforts under way, and I spend my time managing those and count on the teachers and counselors to deal directly with students." In a large high school in a suburban community in Massachusetts, a principal said: "I've been working very hard to organize this faculty and to generate change. I find this taking all of my time, and I haven't found the time to get to know and work with the students."

## Discipline Problems

In response to the discipline question, principals from each kind of community — urban, suburban, rural — reported fighting as a problem among students. Although very well publicized nationally, the presence of guns was noted by only a few of the principals. Security in inner-city schools and in many suburban schools was a concern; therefore many of these schools had security guards, some at the entrance, as well as personnel monitoring the rest of the school grounds.

The most repeated discipline problems for all schools were truancy, cutting classes, and tardiness. Principals in many high schools reported truancy as the major issue.

In an inner-city school in Tennessee, the principal reported that absenteeism was a major problem, caused by youngsters who work 30 hours a week. "They're tired and just miss school. Kids working is a real problem."

A principal in a medium-size school in upstate New York listed his major discipline problems: "Cutting classes, truancy, disruption in classrooms, and failure to do homework."

In high schools in Alabama and Florida, the principals cited fighting among girls as a major discipline problem.

Some principals of inner-city high schools in various locations identified gangs as potential problems. But in several of these schools, principals stated that they had worked with the gangs to make the schools safe havens or, as one said, "neutral turf," and felt they had to some degree contained the problem at the school site.

A number of principals mentioned the presence of drugs. Others echoed the sentiments of one California administrator, who said, "Anyone who feels that there are not some kids using drugs going to his school is kidding himself." Reaction to drugs on campus was swift and brought immediate suspension in all cases.

Although not calling them discipline problems, principals in Arizona, Nebraska, Alabama, and South Carolina identified student apathy and lack of motivation as inhibitors to the education process.

In a large Central Valley high school in California, the principal replied directly, "We have some of everything. Some weapons. Some gangs. Some fights. Some drugs."

A principal in a small rural high school in New Hampshire mentioned the notion of disrespect, as did principals in small, medium, and large high schools in New Mexico, Mississippi, Alabama, South Carolina, and California.

## Characteristics that Make the School "Different"

Although there was a variety of responses to the question of "what qualities or characteristics make this school different from any other," a great number of principals focused on students. Many emphasized their diverse student bodies and how well the students got along as being their major characteristics. Variations of the following statements were repeated frequently:

- "Very reflective of community. We have rich kids; we have poor kids; we have city kids; we have rural kids; we have black kids; we have white kids. The kids are tolerant of each other. They support each other. We don't have a lot of racial problems. Kids come first." (Medium-size urban/suburban school in Florida.)

- "A broader spread of students from different socioeconomic groups than in most schools." (Medium-size urban school in South Carolina.)
- "Diversity of student body. Differences of races, ethnic backgrounds, and how well they get along together." (Large urban high schools in two Southern California cities.)
- "Diverse school ethnically, with large economic differences; but we get along." (Medium-size urban school in an industrial city in Massachusetts.)
- "Diversity of student body and how well we get along. Kids really get along very well." (Medium-size urban/rural school in Arizona.)
- "A diverse group of students. Our top students are particularly achievement oriented. We cut across color lines." (Medium-size Tennessee inner-city high school.)
- "Cosmopolitan and diverse nature of our student body. And that is our strength." (Large urban Nebraska high school.)

The "caring environment" of the school was another student-oriented major characteristic, as noted in the following statements:

- "School slogan is 'A quality education in a caring environment.' We work hard showing the students that we care for them." (Small urban high school in Georgia.)
- "Very positive attitude and atmosphere on campus. Students feel safe. People care." (Medium-size urban school in New Mexico.)
- "We are a caring institution. Put kids number one. A humanistic place to be." (Medium-size urban/rural school in San Joaquin Valley.)
- "A caring faculty, and the kids know this." (Medium-size suburban high school in Oklahoma.)
- "More than anything else, this is a school that cares about kids. It's a warm, safe sanctuary for our kids." (Small Utah city.)
- "Importance of individual. High expectations. Caring relationship with kids. Our school is a safe harbor. Homeroom period reinforces this." (Medium-size urban school in a Southeastern capital city.)
- "This school is a haven for many of the kids, and they know it." (Medium-size Georgia inner-city high school.)
- "We care about kids and exude that in our behavior." (Medium-size school in a small city in Colorado.)

56

- "Where kids know the staff cares." (Small rural town in Wyoming.)

## Primary Goal of the Principal

Almost all the principals stated their primary goals in terms of their students. For example, the principal in a large high school in California's Central Valley said: "To educate kids to be able to deal with a changing technological world. We have been working to restructure to better meet the needs of today's kids."

Change, both among students and in society, was mentioned by a number of principals. The principal of a high school in a large suburb of Los Angeles answered, "To change the way we deliver instruction so it meets the demographic changes that have taken place in this school." Another principal in the same area replied, "To facilitate change to where we have more kids involved in the educational process in ways that make sense to them and to us."

Another theme, mentioned by principals throughout the country, was their desire to prepare their students to take their places in the world as productive citizens, as the following examples indicate:

- "To prepare the students in a well-rounded way to be able to survive in the world after they leave high school. That they have the skills to go to college, to survive academically and socially." (Large suburban high school in upper San Joaquin Valley.)
- "To make sure students get the best education possible. Make sure they are prepared to move out into the world and do whatever they want to do." (Small urban high school in Georgia.)
- "To make sure that the educational program we offer allows a student the best possible education program available. We want them prepared either for higher education or work. We want to meet the needs of kids from all segments of society." (Medium-size suburban school in Kansas.)
- "To have all of our students when they graduate be prepared to enter any post-secondary activity they choose to opt for, whether it be college, the military, or work." (Medium-size urban school in South Carolina.)
- "To increase student expectations, reduce dropout rate, increase number of kids going on to higher education." (Medium-size inner-city school in Colorado.)
- "To help students function well in the society they are going to live in." (Small rural high school in Vermont.)

Recognizing the diversity and varying needs of students, several principals expressed an awareness to meet the needs of all students, not just those who intended to go to college. The following quotes are representative of those made by many principals:

- "To help create a school that meets the needs of all our students." (Large urban/suburban San Joaquin Valley school.)
- "To make our program fully inclusionary to meet the needs of all kids." (Small New England high school.)
- "To raise academic achievement and to have all kids be successful." (Medium-size suburban school in Colorado.)
- "To create a system that truly educates every student so that kids who leave here have the skills to make it in the world." (Medium-size school in Alaska city.)

Many other principals expressed goals similar to that of a principal in a suburban Florida high school, who said, "To provide maximum learning experiences for the students served, and that learning takes place in an environment that is safe and orderly."

The principal in a large Nebraska urban high school simply said: "To make this a student-centered school. Place kids first. We're here to serve kids."

## Most Satisfying Aspects of the Job

As noted in Chapter 4, many principals derived their greatest job satisfaction from their work with teachers. However, the overwhelming majority mentioned their work with students as being the most rewarding part of their job.

The principal of a suburban Los Angeles school summed up a general feeling when he said, "Doing work with kids, staff, or community that improves quality of education on campus." Similar statements were:

- "Interaction with students, also with teachers, but mostly with kids." (Medium-size urban school in Tennessee.)
- "Working with people — kids and staff. Seeing staff and kids succeed." (Medium-size school in a small city in New York.)
- "Working with kids and helping them deal with their problems." (Medium-size suburban/rural school in Nebraska.)
- "Working with kids. They keep me moving. They energize me." (Large high school in a Los Angeles suburb.)

- "Interaction with kids and seeing them do well." (Small town in Oregon.)
- "Interact with students to help them make quality decisions." (Medium-size school in Mississippi city.)
- "Interaction with students." (Small towns in Vermont and New Hampshire.)

A great number of principals said they received the most satisfaction in student success and seeing them graduate. The following statements are typical of many principals:

- "Seeing kids succeed and sharing that joy with staff and kids." (Medium-size Bay Area suburban high school.)
- "See teachers and kids succeed." (Medium-size inner-city school in Tennessee and large city school in San Joaquin Valley.)
- "To really see kids succeeding and know they are happy." (Small urban school in Georgia.)
- "Seeing kids graduate. Feeling you have something to do with their success." (Large suburban Los Angeles high school.)
- "Working with the students and seeing them be successful." (Medium-size urban high school in South Carolina.)
- "Seeing final accomplishments of students. Participating in senior awards ceremony." (Large suburban high school in Southern California.)
- "Day-to-day communication with students. Great pleasure from seeing their successes." (Medium-size urban school in New Mexico.)
- "Positive relations with students. Observing students' success." (Large rural/urban high school in Alabama.)
- "Just knowing you are in a business where you are helping people — kids, teachers. And that is why graduation is such a good experience, because you know that teachers and kids have succeeded." (Large suburban/urban high school in Florida.)
- "To see students succeed. To see a group of kids start in the ninth grade and finish successfully in the senior year. And to have kids come back years later to tell us what we did for them." (Medium-size urban school in Georgia.)
- "Student success at any level and any degree." (Medium-size suburban school in North Carolina.)
- "To see kids, regardless of their backgrounds, have a chance of being who they want to be." (Medium-size urban school in Colorado.)

- "Seeing good things in the classroom. Watching kids light up." (Medium-size rural school in southern San Joaquin Valley.)

Seeing changes in attitudes of students and knowing they were partly responsible for that change brought satisfaction to some principals, as noted in the following quotations:

- "The kids, without a doubt. Seeing them graduate. Seeing them not drop out. Seeing them make good decisions where they used to make bad decisions." (Medium-size urban/suburban school in Florida.)
- "Individual student changing outlook and becoming productive is the most rewarding experience." (Medium-size urban/rural Arizona high school.)
- "End of the year, seeing kids making it — particularly seeing kids who had been on the 'bubble' make it." (Medium-size urban school in New Mexico.)
- "To see students who change their attitudes and graduate from high school, particularly those kids for whom you would not have given a plugged nickel for their chances when they started." (Medium-size rural high school in California.)
- "Watching kids from different socioeconomic groups amalgamate over the year." (Medium-size suburban Arizona school.)
- "Seeing at-risk students achieve and go on to do good things." (Large suburban high school in an agriculture center in San Joaquin Valley.)

## Most Frustrating Aspects of the Job

When asked what was the most frustrating part of the job, the largest percentage of principals found their frustrations resulting from teachers' failure to change and apathetic parents, while only a few saw their frustrations directly related to students.

One principal in a large high school in Tennessee found his most frustrating aspect of the job in student apathy and violence, while a Florida administrator noted his frustration in the school's inability to reach all students. A South Carolina principal reported the poor effort put forth by students to be his major irritation.

The administrator of a Nebraska city high school saw societal changes as they impact students and the family as being his greatest frustration as principal. "We have students living independently, living in cars. They have no role models."

## Conclusions

The overwhelming evidence developed in this study indicated that the principal's major goals and job satisfaction are centered on students. Student success and accomplishment provide much more satisfaction for principals than do such abstractions as meeting district goals and implementing and carrying out restructuring efforts.

The principal spends a great deal of time and energy in direct contact with students. Although much of the interaction is informal — MBWA — he or she often uses other strategies, such as attending student events, tutoring, student forums, and substitute teaching, to get to know the students.

Reading the popular press and watching television could easily lead one to believe that the American high school is a battleground. The interviews and the walks around school buildings, including large urban high schools, presented a very different picture. The principals were keenly aware of the potential for violence and were frank in discussing fighting, drugs, and the occasional presence of arms on campus. Recognizing this potential, principals had as their most important goal to provide a safe learning environment or, as many said, "a haven" for students. Seeing students succeed who come from harsh community environments often was cited as one of the greatest satisfactions of the job.

For all principals, great job satisfaction came from seeing students graduate and be prepared to be productive citizens. Particularly satisfying was seeing students change their attitudes from belligerence or indifference to desire to stay in school and graduate.

chapter six

# COMMUNITY LEADER AND ACTIVIST

After inquiring about the internal workings of the school, I turned attention to school-community relationships. Seeking information about how principals work with the community, I asked three questions that focused directly on the topic.

First I asked, "What is your relationship with the community?" followed by "What structures do you have to facilitate your working relationship with your community?" If principals indicated they did have strategies and structures, I then asked them to describe how they worked with their community.

One further question was asked: "What agencies in the community do you work with most often?"

## Relations with the Community

Experienced principals know their communities well, and newer principals work hard to learn about their communities. Principals know the history and traditions of the school and community. They can describe individual neighborhoods, very much how one would expect an experienced politician to do. In several of the principals' offices, there were detailed street maps of the schools' attendance areas; and the principals could describe each neighborhood and note its ethnic makeup, nature of the housing, SES status, and whether it was stable or in transition. Some mentioned that they periodically drive through the attendance area to see if there are changes and new developments relevant to managing the school.

Very often when describing the quality of their relationship with the community, principals would stress the length of time they had lived there. A principal in a large city in Tennessee stated: "I have excellent relations with my community. I've lived here all of my life. I know everybody, and everybody knows me. For five years I was principal of the middle school that feeds this school, so I had a group of parents who really knew me. There are three schools along this street, and I've been principal of first the elementary, and then the middle school, and now the high school. You could almost say I'm the mayor of the street." Principals throughout the country made similar statements:

- "Fine relations. I live in the community and have for years. My children went to this high school. I'm really a part of the community, and the parents appreciate that." (Medium-size suburban high school in the San Francisco Bay Area.)
- "I'm a long-time resident of the community. In a community of this size, I always run into people from our school community, whether it is a social event, community activity, playing tennis, or just shopping." (Medium-size urban Colorado school.)
- "Very positive. I live in the community and have for many years." (Small high school in a New England college town.)
- "Excellent relations with the community. I've lived here all my life. I was a principal of a junior high school before I took this job, so I got here knowing a good percentage of my parents." (Medium-size urban school in New Mexico.)

Principals who are new to the community are aware of the importance of knowing and working with different elements of the community and try hard to establish relations, as indicated in the following remarks:

- "My relations with the community are developing and growing. I'm new. I spent the first year on the campus dealing with issues here. Now, in my second year, I have begun to reach out, attend community meetings, and work to meet with key community members." (Large urban Southern California school.)
- "I've just started here. I've gone to the churches, worked closely with the PTA, which has been very active, and started a principal's forum that meets once a month and draws up to 300 people. This has given me an opportunity to really meet interested parents and community members." (Medium-size urban school in Mississippi.)
- "Excellent. When I first got here, I worked with the PTA; and we had a series of 'meet-your-principal' sessions at various locations in the community. As the first African-American to be principal of this school, I thought it important that this predominantly white school community get to know who I was and what my commit-

ment and values were. And as long as I have been here, I have had great relations with the community." (Large urban/suburban Florida high school.)

Some principals interacted with the community in unique ways. In a mid-size Nebraska community the principal explained: "We have an open campus, and the kids walk from school to the fast-food places and back. We were getting complaints from people in the neighborhood that students were leaving trash on their lawns and sidewalks. Our administrative team began regular patrols of the area surrounding the school. This put a stop to the trash problem, but it did something else. People saw us, began to chat with us, and, when they got to know us, became real supporters of the school. We asked them if they would like to become patrons of the school, and most agreed. They get the school calendar and an opportunity to buy tickets in advance for important school events."

The principal of a large school in a military town in Southern California replied: "I try hard to work with our different communities. On two sides of the school, we have large mobile home parks that are occupied almost exclusively by service retirees. We would often get complaints about students and noise from athletic events. I began meeting with the presidents of the various neighborhood associations in these mobile home parks. Now we have regular meetings, and we have good understandings. I rarely get complaints anymore."

One administrator in a small South Dakota city had a different role in the community: "I'm really involved with my community. I'm a state legislator, chairman of the House Appropriations Committee. As a result of my political activities, I know just about everybody in this community."

Although most principals stressed the positive nature of their relations with their communities, some felt that the relations could be better. As expressed by a principal in a bedroom community of Los Angeles, "We cover a wide area, and we have a lot of new parents, many of whom commute long distances; and we just have not been able to get them involved."

A principal in a suburb of a large city in Tennessee made a similar statement: "I've just started here, and it seems that parents have never really been involved in this school, nor has the community at large been. No one seems to know why that is the case. But I've been working hard, particularly through our newsletter, to encourage parents to come to school."

In a small Oregon town the principal replied: "Relations are not as close as I would like them to be. I came into what would have to be called a nightmare situation. There had been a lot of turnover with administrators and much community dissension. It is taking people a while to understand that I'm going to be here and I want to work with them and they can trust me."

A principal in a Southwestern capital city said: "We work at it but we just cannot seem to get parents involved. Maybe it is because so many of our kids live so far away from school. We are trying new strategies, and I hope some of them work."

The principal of a large high school in a San Joaquin Valley community said: "We're a very fragmented community. We have a large variety of different ethnic groups that have never worked together, and it has been hard to get them involved in the school."

A Florida city principal answered, "Our community involvement is not as good as I would like it to be. Our community does not like to get involved. We have a lot of rural youngsters mixed in with our urban and suburban students. We have a large attendance area, and our parents just don't get involved. We are doing everything we can think of — such as inviting them to get report cards — but we still have a very poor turnout at school affairs."

Though the nature of the attendance area often was seen as a negative, a small high school in a rural area of Wyoming appeared to have some advantages, as noted in comments from the principal: "I am seen as the key representative of our high school, and I'm asked to speak at public meetings for a great variety of groups — service clubs, church groups, all different kinds of groups. Our school is the community center. Nearly everyone comes to school plays, band concerts, and athletic events. Hundreds of people use our facilities every year."

In the case of a principal in a mid-size North Carolina city, community involvement and support had an interesting payoff: "A few years ago I didn't get along with the superintendent, and I was demoted to a middle-school principalship. The parents and community held a meeting to show their support for me, and 5,000 people showed up. That was just before a board election. The board that demoted me was removed, and shortly thereafter the superintendent was also removed; and I was then reinstated as principal of this school."

## Strategies for Community Involvement

One of the principals' major strategies in working with communities was that of being community activists by having memberships on boards of social agencies and service groups and serving as speakers to such groups, as seen in the following sample of their remarks:

- "I've arranged to speak at one time or another at every service group, community group, and church to explain what we are trying to do at this school." (Medium-size urban school in Mississippi.)
- "I've served and continue to serve on several citywide committees and commissions, and I have chaired several of them. This has enabled me to get to know a lot of people and establish relations with them. I'm a member of a group called Family Connection that develops programs to help parents to work with school and kids together. This has brought me into contact with many community people." (Small urban high school in Georgia.)
- "I've been active in the community and served on many committees citywide that have brought me into contact with a wide spectrum of the community, and the business community in particular." (Medium-size suburban school in Colorado college town.)
- "I'm involved in everything I can get into in the community — whatever it takes to keep good relations with the community." (Large urban high school in Nebraska.)
- "I'm involved in many community clubs and committees, and I work hard at being visible and accessible to everybody." (Small school in Oregon.)
- "I spend a lot of time in the community. I serve on many community boards. I make routine visits to local businesses. I regularly visit the local churches. I make frequent home visits." (Medium-size suburban school in Nebraska.)
- "I've lived in this community for years, and I've been very active. I've been president of the Chamber of Commerce and the Community Development Corporation; and when there was a labor dispute in our local elementary school district, I served as the mediator." (Small town in California's Sacramento Valley.)
- "I meet regularly with the leadership of the NAACP and am often a speaker at the black churches in our community." (Medium-size urban school in San Joaquin Valley city.)
- "I'm chairman of our Community Association on the Arts. I've been a member of Rotary and president." (Small high school in Oregon's Willamette Valley.)

Involvement in the Rotary Club, cited by the Oregon principal, also was mentioned by many other principals. Principals in different states were members of their Rotary Clubs' committees on education. Many principals cited the use of Rotary Club scholarships as an important activity of that group. I visited one school on the day the Rotary was holding its annual career day at that school. The principal told me there were 30 Rotarians representing many occupations and professions who were meeting with students in small groups to talk about careers in their respective fields.

Many principals mentioned speaking at service clubs, again emphasizing Rotary as one of their main links to the community. As a principal in an Alabama city stated, "Although I'm not a member of any service club, I know the leadership of all the clubs in this community; and when I think it appropriate, I get myself invited to speak. And I do this at least once a year with all the service clubs."

One principal in a small Midwestern high school used community involvement in a leadership role to start a program to enable girls who had babies to complete their work toward a high school diploma. "I asked the school board if we could establish a nursery at school so that girls with babies could have a place for them while they went to school. The school board rejected the idea. At the time, I was on the board of the local United Way and on the Social Services Committee of my church; and I turned to these two groups for help. United Way paid for the furniture and classroom equipment, and the church group supported the teacher. After a year of operation, the board changed its mind; and now the effort is a district one."

Working with local churches also was identified as an important strategy to communicate and work with the community. Many principals were active in their churches and felt that this brought them close to the community. As mentioned previously, they sought meetings with churches, particularly those with minority congregations, as important communication techniques.

A principal who was new to a community where he was a member of the predominant religious group said: "I've always been active in my church, and this was a real advantage when I started here, because most of the students in this school and the parents go to this church. I very quickly got to know them, and they got to know me."

Also cited often was working with the charitable arms of various religious groups. Several principals saw the social service programs offered by churches as major supplements to their districts' counseling services. Principals indicated that many such counseling services were available to all students, whether or not they were members of the church supporting such services.

Many principals had specific strategies designed to communicate with parents in a personal way. "I send a personal letter to every youngster who accomplishes something significant," reported one administrator, "and this includes those with 100% attendance per semester and all those who have a grade point average of 3.5 or better. In addition to that, we've established a procedure where teachers tell me when kids have really improved, either in grades, attendance, or discipline; and I send these parents letters, too." Variations of this strategy to communicate positively with parents surfaced in many of the interviews; and the principals emphasized their desire to communicate about the good things students do, rather than only when there are problems in school.

Another principal told me his means of communicating was to attend all school functions — basketball games, plays, musical programs. "This gives me a chance to meet many members of our community and not just parents." Again, this strategy of informal communication was identified by many principals as a means of staying in touch.

At several schools that I visited near Christmas, the principals had prepared Christmas cards with the school logo and had sent them to the parents of every youngster in the school. Personally signing more than 1,500 cards was admittedly a chore, but it served the function of reinforcing the importance of establishing good relations with parents.

A standard strategy for communication was the community newsletter. Sometimes it went to parents of children enrolled in school, but in many instances it was a community newsletter that went to all residents of the area. When asked about funding, principals told me that sometimes the parents furnished the funding and sometimes the school district paid for it. Typically the newsletter urged parents or community members to contact the school with concerns or community issues they thought appropriate.

## Structures to Work with the Community

In many schools the principals used the PTA and booster groups to work with the community. There was also a variety of advisory and governance committees, many of which appeared to be in a developing stage. Getting a handle on the nature of the various advisory groups was difficult. Many appeared to be forming at the principal's initiative, while others were newly emerging as a result of state legislation. The implementation seemed to differ according to the principal's attitude or previous relations with the community.

Samples of common remarks of principals about parent groups follow:

- "We have a variety of parent groups, usually for specific issues; but we also have a PTA and booster clubs." (Medium-size suburban school in California's Central Valley.)
- "We don't have an advisory group, but we have a lot of parent-community involvement. We have a band booster group and also a band alumni group. We have Parents for Jackson High, and they are supported by a school alumni group. Together these two groups raised over $80,000 last year." (Medium-size urban school in Tennessee.)
- "We have a Community Advisory Committee with representatives from all our neighborhoods. We talk about such things as problems that night football games bring to the community that surrounds the school and how we can alleviate the unpleasantness. This advisory committee serves as a forum for anyone from our school neighborhoods to raise concerns they have related to the school." (Large urban/suburban Florida high school.)
- "I have a parent advisory group made up of parents and community members. Anyone can attend our advisory group meetings, but there are bylaws that govern our decision-making process. We also have a club that serves largely as a volunteer group. We're developing a restructuring program; and of the 45 members of the committee, 20 are parents." (Medium-size school in Sacramento Valley.)
- "We have an advisory committee that meets with me monthly, and I work hard to see that all segments of the community are included in this group." (Large suburban high school in a California high desert city.)
- "We have an active PTSA and booster clubs. We also have a Community Advisory Committee made up of local business people and parents. They meet monthly, and we discuss what is going on at school. And they make recommendations." (Mid-size urban school in Georgia.)
- "We have a School Improvement Team that meets once a month comprised of administrators, teachers, and parents. This is not a real decision-making group, but it has a strong influence on what we do. Participation is voluntary, and any parent or community person can be a member. We usually have 20 to 25 people show up." (Medium-size school in rural Colorado community.)

- "We have a Parent Advisory Council. We started this group when I sent out letters to every parent in the school and asked them to participate and got 71 responses. About 25 show up to our meetings, and right now we are working on our agenda and trying to define what we want to do." (Medium-size suburban/rural school in Wyoming.)

Differences in the implementation of a state-mandated governance group can be seen in these statements:

- "We have set up a governance group comprised of parents, students, and teachers. They are supposed to be a decision-making group, and I encourage them to do that." (Medium-size urban school in Massachusetts.)
- "The state-mandated governance group is supposed to have decision-making power; but since I'm responsible and accountable for this school, I reserve the final decisions for myself." (Medium-size suburban school in Massachusetts.)

The community forum was a standard structure in many high schools. I first heard of this in a college town in Oklahoma, and the principal was quite enthusiastic about the effectiveness of this body as a communication strategy. I was to hear about the existence of such a group in many other parts of the country. The forum is not an advisory committee but is a "sounding-board" group. In some schools it appeared to be a no-holds-barred meeting and any issue could be raised, while in other places there were some limitations, particularly as to criticism of specific teachers. Generally, the forums were held one evening a month at an established time and place. In one Southern capital city the principal held them on Sunday afternoons, because this was the time attendees felt it was most convenient for them.

A principal in Canberra, Australia, reported a structure he had organized to involve the community when he had been "brought in to turn the school around" — in other words, to increase the quality of student learning and to improve school climate. The principal organized what he called "cottage meetings" for parents to discuss issues and problems they had concerning the school. He sent notices home requesting that parents in the various neighborhoods of the attendance area make their homes available for groups of 15 to 20 parents so that all parents could attend a meeting within walking distance of their homes. He assigned teachers and administrators to attend these meetings, not as experts but to answer procedural questions about how the school worked. Issues were recorded at each site, and representatives were elected at each site to meet with the principal and to refine the issues into a manageable list. Additional meetings were then called for parents to suggest strategies to address the problems, and solutions were put in priority order and became the basis for the school's improvement plan.

## Minority Outreach Efforts

Many principals devised innovative strategies to involve minority parents. These outreach efforts became so successful that they ultimately resulted in permanent structures for community involvement. Three examples, one from a high school in the San Francisco Bay Area and two from different regions of Colorado, show how some of these efforts were organized and their results.

The California school had a sprawling attendance area where some of the students were bused several miles to and from the school. The principal, with board approval, rented a storefront office in the community. "I'm there every Thursday afternoon from 1:00 to 4:00; and if I can't make it, someone else on our staff is there. It's highly publicized, and we have told the parents it is there for their use. I'll have anywhere from 10 to 15 parents come in during the afternoon, and they have questions on just about anything."

A principal in a rural area of Colorado told of a strategy unique to his circumstance. "We have not been able to get parents from our Indian reservations to come to school, and about 20% of our student population is American Indian. We've gone out to the reservation and used the community center to hold meetings on a variety of topics. The first couple of meetings, no one showed up; but we have persisted and talked to some key Indian leaders to develop an appropriate agenda. Lately the turnout has been better. We're not going to give up. It is important that the Indian community knows we are interested in its children."

In a high school in a large Colorado city with a growing Hispanic population, a group of Hispanic teachers met with the principal and demanded that he work with them to address the problems related to Hispanic low achievement and dropout rates. Working with this group, the principal went out into the community and held meetings in churches, homes, and social agencies to enlist the support of Hispanic parents and the community at large. The principal held 120 meetings at the school, each chaired by a Hispanic parent. These efforts resulted in a school-wide improvement effort with the motto, "This is a school of champions." Displayed in the main reception area of the of the school were pictures of "school champions," about 200 pictures of students who had been nominated as champions for such reasons as markedly improved grades, attendance, or just generally improved attitude. A student picture could be posted for a month or more.

## Involving the Business Community

Many principals were working to involve the business community with the high school. As with so many aspects of the operation of high schools, this involvement took a variety of forms, often based on the nature of the community.

In a South Carolina city the CEO of the headquarters of a major insurance company made the organization's rather lavish meeting rooms regularly available for school meetings and, when appropriate, provided training programs to school managers. In a community in California's high desert, an aircraft company offered its program of Total Quality Management to all high school administrators.

In many instances, companies had career-oriented programs, such as internships, for interested students. In a small town in New Mexico, doctors, lawyers, accountants, and merchants working with the schools established regular programs for students, in some cases having students work alongside the professionals.

Administrators often received contributions from a large variety of local businesses to use as incentives and rewards for students and teachers. One principal noted that faculty meetings were better attended and more fun since local businesses were contributing door prizes, which included certificates for a dinner for two and gift certificates for local shops and hairdressers.

In a school in Wyoming the principal estimated that in one year he had received contributions from local businesses that totaled about $40,000. The gifts included such awards as dinner for two at one of the town's best restaurants for the teacher of the month and an all-expense-paid weekend at a posh ski resort for those who had been voted outstanding teacher or student for a semester.

In several areas, local scientific labs and research centers opened their facilities to selected students. In a suburb of an industrial city in central Massachusetts, top biology students received credit for working in one of the country's major biological concerns. In a community in Georgia, capable science students were given opportunities to work in a regional research hospital.

Principals gave many additional examples of students spending time in an area's businesses. Representative was a mid-size town in New York with a major manufacturing plant, where students and teachers were given the opportunity after hours to use the company's state-of-the-art computers for word processing and spreadsheet and graphics work, computers that would have been far too expensive for the school district to purchase on its own. In this school, teachers spent time at the plant and key executives spent time at the school.

Another emerging community structure is the school foundation. In the past, foundations generally have been districtwide; but I discovered foundations operating at many high schools. In several schools the money raised by foundations became a major supplement to the school budget.

I found an excellent example of the nature of the community and its involvement in the schools in Oklahoma. A new football field and stadium had been completed, but the budget did not include the erection of the towers for lights for night games. The community raised the funds for the standards and the lights; and volunteers from the oil industry, using loaned equipment, put up the standards.

## Community Agencies Worked with Most Often

Community agencies cited as those most often worked with were the police and sheriff's departments and social agencies that deal with problems of children. In several communities, police personnel were assigned full time to individual schools. They played different roles in different locations. In some they were the traditional officer walking the beat, though the corridor, athletic field, gymnasium, parking lot, and cafeteria were the beat. In some schools they conducted classes on such topics as drug and alcohol abuse and the role of law enforcement in the community. The principals were unanimous in their feelings that having the police on campus to meet informally with the kids had improved the school climate and, in many cases, had changed students' attitudes about police.

In small towns the principals often met informally but regularly with representatives from law enforcement to talk about preventive strategies, rather than punitive measures. In many of the large cities, the principals had similar relationships with the local precinct officers.

Principals often cited such social agencies as community mental health services and those agencies responsible for addressing child abuse problems as agencies with which they worked most frequently.

As with the police officers, many principals said they met regularly and informally with social agency people to discuss problems and strategies.

Besides working with the Rotary Club, principals mentioned working with the local chambers of commerce and other business-oriented groups, such as the board of realtors. Some of these groups helped develop scholarships and other positive programs for youth.

## Conclusions

Principals understand the importance of knowing and working with their communities. They understand the relations that various community groups and agencies have with the school and their related impact on what happens in the school. In working with the community, principals are very much like politicians. They know the many neighborhoods and key people from each segment of the community. They understand that relations with various community groups and agencies will have an impact on what happens in the school.

Without violating the traditional tenets advocating separation of church and state, principals often work effectively with the churches and religiously affiliated counseling and social agencies.

Principals seek out leadership roles in the community as a strategy to strengthen the bond with the community and also to enlist such groups as a support network for the schools. They appear as speakers for community groups to maintain their visibility as spokespersons for education.

Varieties of structures are emerging that are intended to involve parents and community members more actively in governance roles that affect school policy. Attitudes among the principals interviewed varied from enthusiastic support of such governance structures to suspicion and reluctance to change traditional roles and relationships.

Where communities are changing, particularly with an increase of minority youngsters in schools, principals see it as one of their major responsibilities to meet the needs of those youngsters and to encourage minority parent involvement in the school.

chapter seven

# LOOKING TO THE FUTURE

Visiting the scores of high schools in the United States and several foreign countries and talking with their administrators have been exciting and rewarding experiences for me. The hospitality shown to me by the principals and their forthright answers to my questions gave me the feeling they liked what they were doing and were confident in how they were performing.

The overall picture I have of America's high schools is a positive one. Their administrators try very hard, often under extremely difficult circumstances and always within the constraints of budget, to provide the environment, resources, and strategies to educate youth of diverse races, cultures, and abilities in a time of great societal change and unrest. They are doing a good job and should be respected for their competence and endurance in the face of constant criticism from exterior voices.

Today's high school principal exudes enormous energy and commitment to providing a safe learning environment for all the students of that school. Although similarities exist among high schools, each principal's situation is unique and depends on the size, age, and traditions of the school, the makeup of the student body and staff, the nature of the community, and the available resources. Each principal recognizes his or her responsibility for what goes on in a school and takes very seriously his or her decision-making power and position as the final arbiter.

The action-oriented leadership of the principal, focused largely on the immediate and day-to-day activities of the school and often without a grand plan or involvement in a restructuring effort, keeps the high school functioning. His or her daily routine is filled with crisis situations, unplanned events that have to be dealt with deftly and immediately while business continues for those not involved. To an outsider, a high school may seem chaotic at times, especially during class changes.

However, it is remarkable that the hundreds of people in a large high school do go about their assigned and varying tasks throughout the day's schedule without more upheaval.

In the interviews with central office personnel and school administrators, I found differences between the district office and school site extremely interesting, reinforcing the notion of isolation of the principal. The exact opposite of the noisy, untidy, bustling school was the dignified atmosphere of the central office, where people quietly went about their work on personnel papers and budgetary documents and were interrupted only occasionally by the ringing of a telephone. Often perceptions of an issue at the central office were completely different from those expressed by principals.

## Some Modest Proposals

I use the term "modest proposals" because, in my interviews, I saw little evidence of dramatic restructuring; and principals expressed little need for dramatic restructuring. In almost all of the schools I visited, the traditional elements of high schools were thriving — the six- or seven-period day, traditional departmental organization, the standard hierarchical arrangement. Further, many principals expressed their feelings that a substantial part of their faculties were not interested in real change and that it would take an inordinate amount of time and effort, or waiting for retirements, to launch real change. Change efforts are necessary. But we should recognize the pragmatic, reality-based view of most principals. Thus I present the following proposals:

*1. Site-based management should become a permanent part of how schools and districts are run.*

I found the movement toward site-based management to be very uneven. And in few schools did I find organized structures established by board policy with a clear set of guidelines calling for a real decision-making structure at the school. To succeed, site-based management must be established by board policy. It requires guidelines to govern the new relationships that will come into existence among personnel at the site level, central office, and board.

In all of the schools where there were identifiable elements of site-based management and principals and staffs felt that they were trusted by the board and superintendent, there was energy, confidence, and commitment. Conversely, where principals felt they were denied this freedom to work with their staffs to shape programs, anger and frustration dissipated their energy and weakened their commitment to what they often felt were irrelevant districtwide goals.

*2. The principal and teachers should spend time talking about changing roles and responsibilities.*

As the principal's role and the domains of decision making change, time has to be spent analyzing how these changes will affect relations with teachers. A structure is necessary to ensure that there will be organized and continued participation of teachers in the process. The structure should be simple and a result of consensus; it should be understood by all members of the faculty and community. This structure also should involve parents. The domains for which this group will assume responsibility — for example, school rules, curriculum, personnel — should be established beforehand. Inservice training should be conducted on such topics as group planning, decision making, and conflict resolution.

Time during the school day is essential for teachers to participate in planning. Evening meetings also might be required to accommodate parents. Time may be made available through more flexible scheduling.

*3. The principal should develop a coherent personal management style based on what he or she is now doing well.*

A personal plan with related strategies could enhance the principal's effectiveness. The principal's practical, down-to-earth approach to the job most often is directed at handling and solving immediate problems, as it should be. But it allows little time for thoughtful reflection on where the school is and where it is going. The development of a personal plan would not eliminate crises, but it could help principals better manage their time.

*4. Each school should have an organized plan for instructional improvement and innovation.*

An organized plan can ensure that instructional improvement and innovation will be school priorities. It also will establish roles and responsibilities for these important activities. Such a plan will define the principal's role as it relates to instructional leadership and innovation.

The evidence presented in this book indicates that the principal's role as an instructional leader often was not clear, nor was his or her role in developing improvement efforts. Many of these efforts appeared to depend on individual teachers and the personal desires of the principal, rather than on organized and sustained efforts. A plan would help the school establish priorities and directions.

5. *The central office must work with principals in establishing new relationships.*

Site-based management will change traditional roles and relationships within schools. The principals in these interviews presented substantial evidence that the functions of school administrators in this new organizational arrangement are changing and that the new relationships often are confusing (see Chapter 2). In turn, site-based management also will change the relationships between the central office and the schools.

Changing the power relationships in schools does not come easily. Time, thought, and open communication are critical for success. An essential element is trust — trust on the part of central office personnel that principals are capable of assuming new responsibilities, and trust on the part of principals that the central office is sincere and committed to the changes.

6. *The principal, district, and teachers must work with unions to ensure that contracts are flexible enough to meet local needs.*

Collective bargaining agreements must be flexible to allow individual schools to meet specific needs at each site. New organizational arrangements and management strategies create conditions that require each school to interpret contract provisions differently. Flexibility in teacher contracts will encourage innovative improvement efforts.

7. *Schools must continue to reach out to all segments of the community, including the business community.*

Almost without exception, the principals I interviewed knew their communities well and established relationships with a variety of community groups. These principals saw working with the community to be as important as working with staff and the central office.

The community must be involved in addressing school problems, such as truancy, dropouts, and graffiti. The community often has many more resources than exist in the schools, and developing relationships with as many segments of the community as possible can only benefit the school.

8. *Schools and universities should work together more closely on research, planning, training, and evaluation.*

The absence of school-university relations, other than cooperating on student teaching, is a major disappointment. Closer working relations would benefit both segments. Spending time in schools, observing teachers and administrators, and participating in problem-solving activities would give greater credibility to university personnel, who often are accused of not being part of the real world. Schools could profit from the university's research and evaluation capabilities, and school and university personnel together could provide sustained and organized inservice programs.

These modest proposals are a reflection of what I saw and learned in the schools I visited. They put the main responsibility for substantive change on the administrators and teachers at each school, because the school is where young people are educated.

The responsibility of leadership for change and improvement should belong to the building principal. If he or she does not lead, no one will. Although central offices can be supportive, they are distant and have only a tangential effect on the day-to-day operation of schools.

I am hopeful, based on the many different efforts to improve education I observed, that many schools are moving in the right direction. Principals will be central to that movement.